Facts for Life

Fourth Edition

World Health Organization

United Nations
Educational, Scientific and
Cultural Organization

UNFPA

UN DP

UNAIDS

JOINT UNITED NATIONS PROGRAMME ON HIV/AIDS

UNHCR UNODC
UNICEF ILO
WFP UNESCO
UNDP WHO
UNFPA WORLD BANK

WFP

World Food Programme

wfp.org

THE WORLD BANK

Facts for Life

CONTENTS

Foreword iv
Purpose vi
Structure vii
Essential Messages. viii
Guide for Using *Facts for Life* x
Glossary. 194

The topics:

Timing Births 1

Safe Motherhood and Newborn Health 11

Diarrhoea 89

Coughs, Colds and More Serious Illnesses 101

Hygiene. 109

Malaria 121

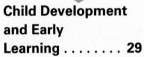

**Child Development
and Early
Learning** **29**

Breastfeeding **47**

**Nutrition
and Growth** **61**

Immunization **77**

HIV **129**

**Child
Protection** **149**

**Injury
Prevention** **163**

**Emergencies:
Preparedness and
Response** **179**

Facts for Life
FOREWORD

Nearly 9 million children died in 2008 from preventable illnesses before reaching their fifth birthday – more than two thirds of them during the first year of life. Millions more survive only to face diminished lives, unable to develop to their full potential.

Five diseases – pneumonia, diarrhoea, malaria, measles and AIDS – together account for half of all deaths of children under 5 years old. Undernutrition is a contributing cause of more than one third of these deaths.

It is possible to save lives and greatly reduce human suffering by expanding low-cost prevention, treatment and protection measures. The challenge is to ensure that this knowledge is shared with parents, caregivers and communities, who are the first line of defence in protecting children from illness and harm.

Facts for Life has been developed as a vital resource for those who need it most. It delivers essential information on how to prevent child and maternal deaths, diseases, injuries and violence.

Since *Facts for Life* was first released in 1989, countless families and communities around the world have put its messages and guidance into practice. These efforts over the years have contributed significantly to progress on key global indicators such as health, education, life expectancy, and infant and maternal morbidity and mortality. Much can be achieved by empowering families and communities to adopt behaviours that improve child survival, growth, learning, development and protection, while also promoting children's and women's rights.

The fourth edition of *Facts for Life* expands on previous editions and contains several significant changes. For example, because of the inextricable link between the health of the mother and the health of the child, a *Newborn Health* section has been included in the *Safe Motherhood* chapter.

A chapter on *Child Protection* has also been added, which focuses on the vulnerabilities of children and the actions needed to ensure that they grow up in supportive environments in the home, school and community.

Facts for Life provides information to help save, improve and protect children's lives, and should be shared widely with families, health workers, teachers, youth groups, women's groups, community organizations, government officials, employers, trade unions, media, and non-governmental and faith-based organizations.

Facts for Life is designed to educate those who have influence over the safety and well-being of children. Through simple messages, it aims to bring life-saving knowledge to every corner of the world.

Ann Veneman
Executive Director
United Nations Children's Fund

Margaret Chan
Director-General
World Health Organization

Koïchiro Matsuura
Director-General
United Nations Educational, Scientific and Cultural
Organization

Thoraya Ahmed Obaid
Executive Director
United Nations Population Fund

Helen Clark
Administrator
United Nations Development Programme

Michel Sidibé
Executive Director
Joint United Nations Programme on HIV/AIDS

Josette Sheeran
Executive Director
World Food Programme

Graeme Wheeler
Managing Director
The World Bank

The Purpose of
FACTS FOR LIFE

Facts for Life aims to provide families and communities with the information they need to save and improve the lives of children. Parents, grandparents, other caregivers and young people can refer to this practical source of information for answers to their questions related to childbearing and getting children off to the best start in life. The challenge is to ensure that everyone **knows and understands** these facts and is motivated to **put them into practice**.

The messages contained in *Facts for Life* are based on the latest scientific findings by medical and child development experts around the world. These facts are presented in simple language so they can be understood and acted upon easily by people without a scientific background. Doing so can save lives.

The *Facts for Life* messages are also based on human rights, particularly the Convention on the Rights of the Child and the Convention on the Elimination of All Forms of Discrimination against Women.

The messages empower people to fulfil the rights of their children. They also are aimed at enabling women, young people and children to exercise and speak out in favour of their rights.

Everyone can help communicate the *Facts for Life* messages — health workers, teachers, social workers, government officials, broadcasters, journalists, community workers, religious and political leaders, mothers, fathers, grandparents, other family members, friends, neighbours, students and people in all walks of life — young and old, men and women, and girls and boys.

The Structure of FACTS FOR LIFE

Facts for Life consists of 14 chapters filled with practical information about how to ensure children's rights to survival, growth, development and well-being. The topics address pregnancy, childbirth, major childhood illnesses, child development, early learning, parenting, protection, and care and support of children.

Each chapter has three parts: an introduction, key messages and supporting information.

THE INTRODUCTION is a brief 'call to action'. It summarizes the extent of the problem and the importance of taking action. The introduction aims to inspire people to get involved and share this information widely. It can be used to motivate political leaders and the mass media.

THE KEY MESSAGES, addressed to parents and other caregivers, are the essence of *Facts for Life.* They contain the essential information that people need to protect their children. The key messages are clear, brief and practical, so people can easily understand them and take the recommended action. These messages are meant to be communicated often and in various ways through multiple channels of communication.

THE SUPPORTING INFORMATION elaborates on each key message, providing additional details and advice. This information is particularly useful for community-based workers, health workers, social workers, teachers and families – anyone who wants to know more about the survival, growth, development and protection of infants and children. It can be used to answer questions from parents and other caregivers.

ESSENTIAL MESSAGES

1. The health of women[1] and children can be significantly improved when births are spaced at least two years between the birth of the last child and the beginning of the next pregnancy. Health risks increase for both the mother and the child when pregnancy occurs before age 18 or after age 35. Both men and women, including adolescents, need to know about the health benefits of family planning so they can make informed choices.

2. All pregnant women should visit a trained health worker for prenatal and post-natal care, and all births should be assisted by a skilled birth attendant. All pregnant women and their families need to know the warning signs of problems during and after pregnancy and the options for seeking assistance. They also need to have plans and resources for obtaining skilled care for the birth and immediate help if problems arise.

3. Children learn from the moment of birth. They grow and learn best when they receive attention, affection and stimulation, in addition to good nutrition and proper health care. Encouraging girls and boys equally to observe and express themselves and to play and explore helps them learn and develop socially, physically, emotionally and intellectually.

4. Breastmilk *alone* is the best food and drink for an infant for the first six months of life. After six months, infants need other nutritious foods, in addition to breastfeeding up to two years and beyond, to meet their growth and development needs.

5. Poor nutrition during the mother's pregnancy or the child's first two years can slow a child's mental and physical development for life. Children need a well-balanced diet that includes protein and energy foods as well as vitamins and minerals, such as iron and vitamin A, to ensure good health and development. From birth to age 1, children should be weighed every month and from age 1 to age 2, at least every three months. If a child does not appear to be growing, the child should be seen by a trained health worker.

6. Every child should complete the recommended series of immunizations. Immunizations during a child's first year of life and into the second year are especially important for early protection against diseases that can cause poor growth, disability or death. All women of childbearing age, including adolescent girls, need to be protected against tetanus for their own benefit and for their future babies. Over time, five doses of tetanus vaccine are recommended for lifelong protection. A booster should be given during pregnancy if the woman has not yet received five doses.

7. A child with diarrhoea needs plenty of the right liquids — breastmilk and ORS (oral rehydration salts) solution – and, if older than 6 months, other nutritious liquids and foods should be added. Zinc should be given to reduce the severity of the diarrhoea.

---

1   Throughout this publication, references to pregnant women include pregnant adolescents.

If the diarrhoea is mixed with blood or is frequent and watery, the child is in danger and should be taken to a trained health worker for immediate treatment.

8. Most children with coughs or colds will get better on their own. But if a child with a cough and fever is breathing rapidly or with difficulty, the child is in danger and needs to be taken to a trained health worker for immediate treatment.

9. Many illnesses can be prevented by good hygienic practices: washing hands with soap and water (or a substitute, such as ash and water) after defecating or cleaning a child who has defecated, using clean toilets or latrines, disposing of faeces away from play and living areas and water sources, washing hands before handling food, using water from a safe source, disinfecting drinking water if its safety is in question, and keeping food and water clean.

10. Malaria, which is transmitted through mosquito bites, can be fatal. Wherever malaria is present, people should sleep under insecticide-treated mosquito nets; any child with a fever should be examined by a trained health worker for treatment and sponged gently with cool (not cold) water; and pregnant women should take antimalarial tablets as recommended by a trained health worker.

11. HIV (human immunodeficiency virus), the virus that causes AIDS (acquired immunodeficiency syndrome), is preventable and treatable, but incurable. HIV is transmitted through unprotected sex with an HIV-infected person; transmission from an HIV-infected mother to her child during pregnancy, childbirth or breastfeeding; and blood from HIV-contaminated syringes, needles or other sharp instruments and transfusion with HIV-contaminated blood. Educating all people on HIV and reducing stigma and discrimination should be part of the information, education and communication on HIV prevention, testing and care. Early diagnosis and treatment of children and adults can better ensure their survival and a longer and healthier life. Children and families affected by HIV should have access to child-friendly health and nutritional care and social welfare services. All people living with HIV should know their rights.

12. Girls and boys should be equally protected within their family, school and community. If these protective environments are lacking, children are more vulnerable to violence, abuse, sexual exploitation, trafficking, child labour, harmful practices and discrimination. Living with family, birth registration, access to basic services, protection from violence, a child-friendly justice system based on child rights, and children's active engagement in developing their knowledge and skills to protect themselves are important building blocks in constructing protective environments in which children can develop and fulfil their potential.

13. Many serious injuries that can result in disabilities or death can be prevented if parents or other caregivers watch young children carefully, keep their environment safe and teach them how to avoid accidents and injuries.

14. Families and communities must prepare for emergencies. In disasters, conflicts, epidemics or pandemics, children and women must be the first to receive attention, including essential health care, adequate nutrition, support for breastfeeding and protection from violence, abuse and exploitation. Children should have access to recreation and learning opportunities in safe, child-friendly schools and spaces that give them a sense of normalcy and stability. Children should be cared for by their parents or other familiar adults, so that they feel secure.

Guide for Using
FACTS FOR LIFE

Using *Facts for Life* can increase people's knowledge and change their practices and behaviour to improve and save children's lives. This can lead to positive changes in social beliefs and norms (what is considered normal by society) concerning the survival, growth, learning, development, protection, care and support of children.

Facts for Life is both a practical source of information for individuals and an essential tool for empowering individuals, young people, families and communities. Its messages and information can promote dialogue, learning and communication among children, youth, families, communities and social networks.

People from all walks of life can drive social change in favour of children's rights. Working together can make it possible to find diverse, relevant, interesting and constructive ways of using and communicating *Facts for Life* messages far and wide.

This guide for using *Facts for Life* provides:

- some conceptual thinking on the process of behavioural and social change
- information on using formative research and assessment to measure behaviour change
  - research determines 'baseline' behaviours for use in helping to design and plan an intervention or campaign aimed at changing behaviours
  - assessment measures behaviour changes against the 'baseline' behaviours during or following implementation of an intervention or campaign
- practical guidance on how to use *Facts for Life* to promote behaviour and social change that favours children's right to survive, grow, learn, develop and achieve their full potential in life.

Changing behaviours

Knowledge alone is insufficient for behaviour change

It is often assumed that if people are provided with information, products (such as vaccines or handpumps) and services (such as health or education), they will adopt healthier behaviours.

However, information, products and services are often not enough to ensure adoption of new behaviours.

It is important to go beyond giving people information. *Facts for Life* should be used in consultation with children, families, communities and social networks. Their participation is vital to influencing behavioural and social change in favour of children's rights. Using *Facts for Life* as a tool in communication and development interventions involves:

- listening to the concerns of children, families and communities about the topics in *Facts for Life*
- communicating the messages and supporting information in *Facts for Life* in interesting and constructive ways that are relevant to a particular context
- stimulating dialogue among all concerned
- supporting actions with children, families and communities that improve behaviours related to the topics in *Facts for Life*
- assessing the actions to determine behaviour change and outcomes.

Stages of behaviour change

As individuals, we go through different stages in changing our behaviour. These stages include:

- not being aware
- becoming aware
- becoming motivated to try something new
- adopting a new behaviour
- sustaining and 'internalizing' a new behaviour so that it becomes part of our normal everyday practice.

First, we have to become aware that a particular behaviour may not be healthy for us or our children. We then learn that there are other choices or alternative behaviours. We decide to try a new behaviour. If we are satisfied that the new behaviour is beneficial we may repeat it. Ultimately, we may adopt it. Then we may advocate or promote it with others, encouraging them to adopt it too.

Learning a new behaviour takes place in this continual cycle of awareness, experimentation and repetition. For example, a father may be persuaded through talking with the local religious leader to have his children sleep under insecticide-treated mosquito nets. He then sees that the nets prevent mosquito bites and that his children do not get malaria. He becomes an advocate for sleeping under insecticide-treated mosquito nets, sharing his experience with friends and urging them to use the nets.

Sometimes people who appear to have adopted a new behaviour eventually reject it and return to their former behaviour. For example, the father who was promoting use of mosquito nets may start to feel that they are too much trouble, so he and his family members stop using them. Returning to this old behaviour can harm the health of his family.

Ensuring the adoption of a new behaviour that benefits children and families requires an integrated and sustained communication and development strategy. This involves using different messages and methods to support the 'change continuum' of adopting the new behaviour by individuals and families. The new behaviour may gradually be adopted by the whole community so that, for example, everyone is using insecticide-treated mosquito nets.

Behaviour change creates a dynamic that may result in social change

Individuals rarely change all by themselves. Their behaviour often depends on and is influenced by the views and practices of their families, friends and communities. Sometimes these are positive, as when everybody washes their hands with soap and water after using the toilet or latrine. Other times they may be harmful, as when parents have their daughters undergo genital cutting or refuse to have their children vaccinated.

To change social behaviour means changing the everyday views and practices of families and communities. What parents, other caregivers, children and adolescents decide to do is often influenced by what others are doing around them.

Resistance can be expected when social norms are challenged. This is because change involves shifting the dynamics of a group on fundamental issues related to gender roles, power relations and many other factors within the family or community.

But acceptance can become contagious when society begins to see the economic and social benefits of adopting a new behaviour. An example is when families using mosquito nets no longer have to cope with sickness or death caused by malaria. Their energies can be directed to sustain their children's learning and the family's productivity. People begin to see and hear about the change, and interest spreads, prompting others to adopt the new behaviour that can benefit their lives. Eventually, the behaviour is considered normal practice by everyone.

The Malawi Interfaith AIDS Association has integrated verses and teachings from the *Holy Bible* and the *Holy Quran* into *Facts for Life* booklets used during sermons in churches and mosques.

Facts for Life is also used by community radio stations and television stations, and in *Boma Lathu*, a newsletter in the local language. The village heads use *Facts for Life* for community reading sessions.

Knowing the 'baseline' behaviours

Conduct formative research to establish the 'baseline' behaviour(s)

Formative research is important in the design and planning stages of programming. It helps to clarify the current situation and develop the objectives and baseline behaviour information needed for subsequent measurement of behaviour change following intervention(s). In so doing, it helps those involved and participating in the programming identify and understand interests and concerns, reasons for specific behaviours, and what particular needs and areas of child rights are inadequately addressed.

Conducting formative research involves the gathering, review, analysis and synthesis of available demographic, health, education, sociocultural, political, economic, and media and communication-related data and information using a range of qualitative and quantitative research methods. Research outcomes are best when the data and information are gender disaggregated and related to child rights/human rights. Using a gender lens and a human rights approach can increase awareness and improve and deepen understanding of practices and behaviours affecting girls and boys and their families and communities.

In Cameroon, *Facts for Life* messages, translated into Foufoulde, Gwaya, Haoussa and Pidgin and accompanied by related images, are used in the schools by the local communication groups (Cellules locales de communication) and Mothers' Associations (Associations des mères d'élèves).

It is important that the research involve the participation of children, families, communities and researchers in order to collectively determine the actions necessary to change behaviours to realize children's rights. Research can be organized and conducted by local academic institutions or research firms.

Use formative assessment to measure behavioural change

Formative assessment during and following implementation of interventions provides updates on changes in the behaviours of individuals and families and even entire communities. The behavioural changes can be measured against the baseline behaviours.

Simple research methods, such as surveys and focus group discussions, are an important part of formative research and assessment. They can help ensure that local behaviour is well understood and that chosen actions are supported collectively. Extra attention should be given to ensure inclusion of the opinions of girls and boys, young people and women.

Establishing the baseline behaviours can make it easier to systematically and effectively monitor and evaluate interventions and desired behaviour changes and outcomes. The findings can help to produce constructive conclusions and recommendations for making timely and strategic changes in programming.

Communicating *Facts for Life* messages

Examine the messages and supporting information in* Facts for Life, and, if necessary, adapt them to the local situation. Translate them where necessary. Effectively communicate the messages and facilitate dialogue.***

The text in *Facts for Life* should be examined and, if necessary, adapted in collaboration with authorities (health, education, social services and so forth) to take into account locally relevant issues. This should be done in consultation with family and community members.

In facilitating communication and dialogue with participant groups on the messages, give attention to the following:

- Ensure consideration of gender issues. In some settings, women may not be empowered to make decisions about their children's care or their own, or men may not be encouraged to participate in child care and household chores.

- Raise attention on children's rights to help the participant group identify and become aware of behaviours related to children's health, nutrition, development, education and protection that may have been overlooked.

- Involve children and young people in the dialogue on the messages and information as well as the planning and use of *Facts for Life*. Support peer-to-peer approaches and different methods to increase child participation.

- When adapting or translating the messages and information, use simple language and illustrations that people understand. Do not overload the messages with too many actions or technical details.

> In Honduras, a radio broadcast about a new ORS (oral rehydration salts) product neglected to mention that it was for children suffering from diarrhoea (locally called *empacho*). Mothers and fathers did not understand it was a treatment for *empacho* because the word was not used. This underlines the necessity of pretesting messages.

- Make sure the participant group understands the messages and information and knows how to put them into practice. If materials have been developed in a participatory manner, this will be more easily done.

- Always pretest the messages and illustrations with groups of people for whom they are intended. This can be done by asking the test groups open-ended questions and encouraging discussion to determine whether each message is clearly understood.

- Repetition is vital! Most people do not learn or change behaviour after only one discussion or exposure to a new behaviour.

- Select communication channels that are most effective in reaching the participant groups. Use existing channels and do not rely on a single means of communication. Use a mix of interpersonal; community, traditional and 'mid' media; and mass media so that people receive and discuss the messages repeatedly and in many variations and circumstances. (*Refer to the following section entitled* Use a mix of communication channels.)

Give people the opportunity to discuss, shape and absorb new information for themselves and their communities

People are more likely to trust information and to act on it to change behaviours if:

- they are encouraged to discuss it among themselves and to ask questions to clarify their understanding

- they understand how they and their families and communities will benefit

- the language is familiar and compatible with the local culture and social norms, avoiding judgemental or prescriptive-sounding 'orders'

- the person presenting it or the source of information (such as radio or television) is well known and trusted

- they hear repeated, simple and consistent messages from different sources

- they are given time to change, especially if the change carries a cost, such as installation of latrines.

> In Senegal, *Facts for Life* messages have been used to promote exclusive breastfeeding, curb the spread of cholera, advocate for the abandonment of female genital cutting and encourage skin-to-skin contact between mothers and newborns (especially for premature babies), in addition to other baby-care practices.

Use a mix of communication channels: interpersonal; community, traditional and 'mid' media; and mass media

Interpersonal: person-to-person

Most people are not comfortable using new information seen or heard in the mass media without having an opportunity to discuss it with someone they trust. Person-to-person communication, supplemented by mass and traditional and/or 'mid' media campaigns and ongoing programming activities, are most effective in encouraging people to adopt, sustain and internalize new behaviours.

Using *Facts for Life* effectively requires facilitating participant groups, especially the most marginalized, to become engaged in meaningful dialogue. It is important to reach remote communities, children with disabilities and minority or indigenous children and families. It is also vital that women and girls participate as fully as men and boys.

To facilitate an interpersonal discussion:

- Use simple examples of problems that are important to the people involved. Start with what is already known and focus on major concerns. Avoid technical or scientific language. Use illustrations to stimulate discussion.

- Encourage people to ask questions and express concerns. Guide the discussion to explore the causes of the problem and possible solutions. Remember to listen, which is as important to communication as speaking. The participation of children, families and other community members is key to identifying barriers or unforeseen problems that prevent people from acting on the message. They can articulate local solutions.

- Show respect for people's opinions, knowledge and ability to change. People learn best in situations that build their confidence, and they take action when they feel understood and respected. Be a role model for the behaviour you would like to see adopted.

- Support people in taking action. Recognize that they may want to change but may not be able to act alone. Help them mobilize existing networks or create new ones that will encourage more individuals and families to adopt and sustain new behaviours.

Community, traditional and 'mid' media

This type of communication refers to materials or communication methods that are in between the person-to-person approach and the mass audience approach. Some examples include:

- Street theatre: Used to deliver key messages by a small group of actors for groups ranging from a few dozen to hundreds of people.

- Cell phone messages: Used to urge parents or other caregivers to take their children for their vaccinations, etc.

- Internet: Used for communication and as a source of information. The internet is expanding rapidly and is particularly familiar to adolescents and young people, from urban areas to remote villages; websites such as YouTube are especially popular.

- Posters, leaflets and badges or buttons: Often used to reinforce information communicated through interpersonal contact or social mobilization efforts.

- Videos and audio cassettes: Used to effectively broadcast messages through mobile vans and community TV viewing groups.

- Poetry, song and puppetry: Especially used to engage children and youth.

- Slide sets and flip charts: Often used in community centres and schools.

Bangladesh has been using messages from *Facts for Life* for nearly 20 years. Known as *Shasthyo Tothyo* in Bengali, it has become a household name over the years.

The messages communicated through many materials and media have been widely disseminated by and among government officials, NGOs, teachers, community workers, medical students, child rights committees, women's organizations, local authorities, health workers, nurses, artists and theatre groups.

Facts for Life messages have even shaped curriculum content – once a week, many primary schools have one class dedicated to information from *Facts for Life*.

Mass media

Mass media (radio, newspapers and television) are excellent tools for reaching large numbers of people to introduce and reinforce new information and promote a particular social change. Some steps include:

- Assist participant groups in identifying their primary mass media channels. *What is the source of their information and news?* If community radio is as important to them as national radio, find ways to work with local radio networks.

- Publicize the same message in various media. Repetition reinforces behaviour change, strengthens memory and enhances learning. This helps people retain the message and encourages them to act on it. Examples of media channels include interviews, news articles, round-table discussions, radio or television dramas, soap operas, puppet shows, comics, jingles or songs, quizzes, contests and call-in shows.

- Understand who in the household makes decisions about what to listen to or watch, and make sure the message targets them.

- If the messages are aired on radio or television, make sure they are broadcast at a time when families are listening or watching. Do not rely only on free public service announcements aired during off-peak hours.

- Broadcast messages during popular programmes so they reach a wide audience. Ask popular disc jockeys and television show hosts to discuss the messages on radio call-in programmes or TV shows with live audiences.

India's number one television drama series, *Kyunki Jeena Issi Ka Naam Hai*, is based on *Facts for Life*. Launched in 2008, the series reaches 56 million viewers who are mostly women between 15 and 34 years old.

The show communicates *Facts for Life* messages through engaging stories. Viewers relate the experiences of the characters to their own lives.

Assessments in some states have revealed that midwives have been so inspired by the show's popular nurse character that they feel more motivated in their work. *Facts for Life* messages have also reinforced the midwives' knowledge, for example, regarding prenatal check-ups.

Use of mixed communication methods produces the best results

To achieve behaviour change that favours the rights of all children, it is key to use a mix of communication channels, combining short-term, campaign-style actions with long-term and interactive communication.

Refer to the Facts for Life *website, **www.factsforlifeglobal.com**, for further information on communication for development and a collection of supplementary resources related to each of the chapters.*

Why it is important to share and act on information about
TIMING BIRTHS

Too many births, births too close together and births to adolescent girls under 18 and women over 35 endanger the lives of women and adolescents and their infants.

Family planning is one of the most effective ways to improve women's and children's health and survival. Family planning services provide women and men with information, education and the means to plan when to begin having children, how many to have, how far apart to have them and when to stop. However, millions of women of childbearing age, including adolescent girls, do not have control over limiting pregnancies or spacing births, nor do they have access to effective family planning methods.

Both women and men have the right to choose how many children to have and when to have them. With family planning services they are enabled to make informed decisions on pregnancy by taking into account the benefits and risks, including those related to age and level of access to health services.

Ensuring access to family planning services for women and men, and to education for all children would help prevent many maternal and child deaths and disabilities, particularly in countries where marriage occurs early in life. Together these measures can contribute to women's, adolescent girls' and children's right to survival, health and well-being.

KEY MESSAGES:
What every family and community
has a right to know about

TIMING BIRTHS

1. Pregnancy before the age of 18 or after the age of 35 increases the health risks for the mother and her baby.

2. For the health of both mothers and children, a woman should wait until her last child is at least 2 years old before becoming pregnant again.

3. The health risks of pregnancy and childbirth increase if a woman has had many pregnancies.

4. Family planning services provide men and women of childbearing age with the knowledge and the means to plan when to begin having children, how many to have, how far apart to have them and when to stop. There are many safe, effective and acceptable methods of planning for and avoiding pregnancy.

5. Both men and women, including adolescents, are responsible for family planning. Both partners need to know about the health benefits of family planning and the available options.

TIMING BIRTHS

KEY MESSAGE

1. Pregnancy before the age of 18 or after the age of 35 increases the health risks for the mother and her baby.

SUPPORTING INFORMATION

Every year over 500,000 women die from pregnancy and childbirth complications. For every woman who dies, approximately 20 more develop infections and severe disabling problems – adding up to more than 10 million women affected each year. Access to and use of family planning services could prevent many of these deaths and disabilities.

Delaying a first pregnancy until a girl is at least 18 years of age helps to ensure a safer pregnancy and childbirth. It reduces the risk of her baby being born prematurely and/or underweight. This is especially important where early marriage is the custom and married adolescents face pressure to become pregnant.

Childbirth is more likely to be difficult and dangerous for an adolescent than for an adult. Babies born to very young mothers are much more likely to die in the first year of life. Young adolescents do not yet have a fully developed pelvis. Pregnancy for them can result in serious consequences, such as eclampsia, premature labour, prolonged labour, obstructed labour, fistula, anaemia (thin blood) or infant and/or maternal death.

The younger the mother is, the greater the risk to her and her baby. The risk of maternal death related to pregnancy and childbirth for adolescent girls between 15 and 19 years of age accounts for some 70,000 deaths each year. For adolescents under 15 years of age these risks increase substantially. Girls who give birth before age 15 are five times more likely to die in childbirth than women in their twenties.

Adolescent girls and young women, married or unmarried, need special help to delay pregnancy. All who might be involved with an early pregnancy – adolescent girls and young women and adolescent boys and men as well as their families – should be aware of the risks involved and how to avoid them. This should include information on how to prevent sexually transmitted infections (STIs), including HIV.

After the age of 35, the health risks associated with pregnancy and childbirth begin to increase again. The risks may include hypertension (high blood pressure), haemorrhage (loss of blood), miscarriage and gestational diabetes (diabetes during pregnancy) for the woman and congenital anomalies (birth defects) for the child.

Throughout this publication, references to pregnant women include pregnant adolescents.

It is important to note that the pregnant adolescent is at increased risk of pregnancy complications such as eclampsia, premature labour, prolonged labour, obstructed labour, fistula, anaemia and death.

For her baby, there is a greater risk of premature birth, low birthweight, health problems and death.

For the pregnant adolescent under 15 years of age, these risks increase substantially.

KEY MESSAGE

2.

For the health of both mothers and children, a woman should wait until her last child is at least 2 years old before becoming pregnant again.

SUPPORTING INFORMATION

The risk of death for newborns and infants increases significantly if the births are not spaced. There is a higher chance that the new baby will be born too early and weigh too little. Babies born underweight are less likely to grow well, more likely to become ill and four times more likely to die in the first year of life than babies of normal weight.

One of the threats to the health and growth of a child under age 2 is the birth of a sibling. For the older child, breastfeeding may stop, and the mother has less time to prepare the foods and provide the care and attention the child needs.

Whenever a new baby comes into the family, it is important for the father to help the mother with the new baby and the other children. Both mothers and fathers and other caregivers should give equal attention and care to both girls and boys.

A mother's body needs time to recover fully from pregnancy and childbirth. She needs to regain her health, nutritional status and energy before she becomes pregnant again.

If a woman has a miscarriage or abortion, she should wait at least six months before becoming pregnant again in order to reduce the risk to herself and her baby.

To protect the health of their families, men as well as women need to be aware of the importance of (1) a two-year space between the birth of the last child and the beginning of the next pregnancy and (2) the need to limit the number of pregnancies.

KEY MESSAGE

3.

The health risks of pregnancy and childbirth increase if a woman has had many pregnancies.

SUPPORTING INFORMATION

A woman's body can easily become exhausted by repeated pregnancies, childbirth and caring for small children. After many pregnancies, she faces an increased risk of serious health problems such as anaemia and haemorrhage.

KEY MESSAGE

4. Family planning services provide men and women of childbearing age with the knowledge and the means to plan when to begin having children, how many to have, how far apart to have them and when to stop. There are many safe, effective and acceptable methods of planning for and avoiding pregnancy.

SUPPORTING INFORMATION

Trained health workers and clinics should offer information and advice to empower women to make decisions about family planning and to help women and men choose a family planning method that is acceptable, safe, convenient, effective and affordable.

Trained health workers and clinics should also provide adolescent girls and boys with reproductive health information and family planning services that are (1) sensitive to adolescents and (2) geared to help them develop their skills to make healthy and responsible life decisions.

Special channels to reach out to adolescent girls and pregnant adolescents need to be developed to provide them with support which may include counselling, contraceptives, and prenatal and post-natal services. Pregnant adolescents require special attention and more frequent visits to the health clinic for prenatal and post-natal care.

Adolescent boys and men can play a key role in preventing unplanned (unintended) pregnancies. It is important that they have access to information and services related to sexual and reproductive health.

The more formal education an adolescent girl or woman has, the more likely she is to use reliable family planning methods, delay marriage and childbearing, be better off economically and have fewer and healthier babies. Enrolling and keeping girls in school is therefore extremely important for maternal and child health, in addition to all the other benefits of education.

Of the various contraceptive methods, only condoms protect against both pregnancy and sexually transmitted infections, including HIV.

It is critical to educate adolescent boys, young men and men on their responsibility regarding condom use. Adolescent girls and boys, married or unmarried, need to know about the dual protection of a condom and another kind of contraception (using two methods of contraception at the same time) to help avoid pregnancy and prevent sexually transmitted infections (STIs), including HIV.

In some countries, deaths related to abortion are high among adolescent girls. Adolescent girls, young women and their partners should be provided with information on pregnancy prevention and the risks associated with abortion.

A mother who feeds her baby *only* with breastmilk, on demand day and night during the baby's first six months, can delay the return of menstruation and help prevent pregnancy. There is a small chance that she can become pregnant before her periods return. The risk is less than 2 per cent, which is similar to that of other family planning methods. However, this risk increases after six months.

KEY MESSAGE

5.

Both men and women, including adolescents, are responsible for family planning. Both partners need to know about the health benefits of family planning and the available options.

SUPPORTING INFORMATION

Men and women, including adolescents, must take responsibility for preventing unplanned pregnancies. They should seek advice and have access to information from a trained health worker on the various methods and benefits of family planning.

Information can be obtained from a doctor, nurse, midwife, maternity centre or family planning clinic. In some places, a teacher, a youth organization or a women's organization may also be able to provide this information.

Why it is important to share and act on information about SAFE MOTHERHOOD AND NEWBORN HEALTH

Every pregnant woman hopes for a healthy baby and an uncomplicated pregnancy. However, every day, about 1,500 women and adolescent girls die from problems related to pregnancy and childbirth. Every year, some 10 million women and adolescent girls experience complications during pregnancy, many of which leave them and/or their children with infections and severe disabilities.

Each year, about 3 million babies are stillborn, and 3.7 million babies (latest data available, 2004) die very soon after birth or within the first month. The poor health of the mother, including diseases that were not adequately treated before or during pregnancy, is often a factor contributing to newborn deaths or to babies born too early and/or with low birthweight, which can cause future complications.

The risks of childbearing for the mother and her baby can be greatly reduced if: (1) a woman is healthy and well nourished before becoming pregnant; (2) she has regular maternity care by a trained health worker at least four times during every pregnancy; (3) the birth is assisted by a skilled birth attendant, such as a doctor, nurse or midwife; (4) she and her baby have access to specialized care if there are complications; and (5) she and her baby are checked regularly during the 24 hours after childbirth, in the first week, and again six weeks after giving birth.

Pregnant women and their partners who are HIV-positive or think they may be infected should consult a trained health worker for counselling on reducing the risk of infecting the baby during pregnancy, childbirth and breastfeeding, and caring for themselves and their baby.

Governments have a responsibility to ensure that every woman has access to quality maternity care, including prenatal and post-natal services; a skilled birth attendant to assist at childbirth; special care and referral services in the event serious problems arise; and maternity protection in the workplace.

Most governments have ratified the Convention on the Elimination of All Forms of Discrimination against Women. Some countries have ratified the international agreements on maternity protection, and most have enacted legislation on maternity protection. These international agreements in defence of women's rights include a legally binding commitment to provide pregnant women and mothers with health services and protection in the workplace.

Many women, including adolescents, have difficulty accessing quality health care due to poverty, distance, lack of information, inadequate services or cultural practices. Governments and local authorities, with support from non-governmental and community-based organizations, have a responsibility to address these issues to ensure that women receive the quality health care they need and that they and their newborns have a right to receive.

SAFE MOTHERHOOD AND NEWBORN HEALTH

1. Girls who are educated and healthy and who have a nutritious diet throughout their childhood and teenage years are more likely to have healthy babies and go through pregnancy and childbirth safely if childbearing begins after they are 18 years old.

2. The risks associated with childbearing for the mother and her baby can be greatly reduced if a woman is healthy and well nourished before becoming pregnant. During pregnancy and while breastfeeding, all women need more nutritious meals, increased quantities of food, more rest than usual, iron-folic acid or multiple micronutrient supplements, even if they are consuming fortified foods, and iodized salt to ensure the proper mental development of their babies.

3. Every pregnancy is special. All pregnant women need at least four prenatal care visits to help ensure a safe and healthy pregnancy. Pregnant women and their families need to be able to recognize the signs of labour and the warning signs of pregnancy complications. They need to have plans and resources for obtaining skilled care for the birth and immediate help if problems arise.

4. Childbirth is the most critical period for the mother and her baby. Every pregnant woman must have a skilled birth attendant, such as a midwife, doctor or nurse, assisting her during childbirth, and she must also have timely access to specialized care if complications should occur.

5. Post-natal care for the mother and child reduces the risk of complications and supports mothers and fathers or other caregivers to help their new baby get a healthy start in life. The mother and child should be checked regularly during the first 24 hours after childbirth, in the first week, and again six weeks after birth. If there are complications, more frequent check-ups are necessary.

6. A healthy mother, a safe birth, essential newborn care and attention, a loving family and a clean home environment contribute greatly to newborn health and survival.

7. Smoking, alcohol, drugs, poisons and pollutants are particularly harmful to pregnant women, the developing fetus, babies and young children.

8. Violence against women is a serious public health problem in most communities. When a woman is pregnant, violence is very dangerous to both the woman and her pregnancy. It increases the risk of miscarriage, premature labour and having a low-birthweight baby.

9. In the workplace, pregnant women and mothers should be protected from discrimination and exposure to health risks and granted time to breastfeed or express breastmilk. They should be entitled to maternity leave, employment protection, medical benefits and, where applicable, cash support.

10. Every woman has the right to quality health care, especially a pregnant woman or a new mother. Health workers should be technically competent and sensitive to cultural practices and should treat all women, including adolescent girls, with respect.

SAFE MOTHERHOOD AND NEWBORN HEALTH

1. **Girls who are educated and healthy and who have a nutritious diet throughout their childhood and teenage years are more likely to have healthy babies and go through pregnancy and childbirth safely if childbearing begins after they are 18 years old.**

SUPPORTING INFORMATION

Girls with more formal education are better equipped to fulfil their potential in life. They tend to know about health-care practices and are less likely to become pregnant at a very young age. They are more likely to marry later, have fewer and better-spaced pregnancies, and seek prenatal and post-natal care. It is estimated that two maternal deaths can be prevented for every additional year of school attendance per 1,000 women.

The healthy growth and development of a girl through adolescence helps to prepare her for healthy pregnancies during her childbearing years.

In addition to education and health care, girls need a nutritious diet during childhood and adolescence to reduce problems later in pregnancy and childbirth. A nutritious diet includes iodized salt and foods rich in essential minerals and vitamins such as beans and other pulses, grains, green leafy vegetables, and red, yellow and orange vegetables and fruits. Whenever possible, milk or other dairy products, eggs, fish, chicken and meat should be included in the diet.

Girls who stay in school are more likely to delay marriage and childbirth. Early pregnancy can have serious consequences for adolescents under 18 years old, particularly for those under 15 years old. Adolescent girls and their babies are at much higher risk of complications and death.

It is important to empower girls to avoid early pregnancy and inform both girls and boys about the risks of early pregnancy as well as sexually transmitted infections, including HIV. They both need to develop the skills to make healthy life choices that also support equality and respect in relationships.

Genital cutting of girls and women can cause severe vaginal and urinary infections that can result in sterility or death. It can also cause dangerous complications during childbirth.

Health workers and community outreach programmes can help raise awareness of harmful practices and the importance for adolescents to delay marriage and pregnancy for their health and well-being.

Families need to understand the high risks of early pregnancy. If an adolescent girl marries early and/or becomes pregnant, her family should provide her with support and ensure she obtains the health services she needs.

KEY MESSAGE

2.

The risks associated with childbearing for the mother and her baby can be greatly reduced if a woman is healthy and well nourished before becoming pregnant. During pregnancy and while breastfeeding, all women need more nutritious meals, increased quantities of food, more rest than usual, iron-folic acid or multiple micronutrient supplements, even if they are consuming fortified foods, and iodized salt to ensure the proper mental development of their babies.

SUPPORTING INFORMATION

Adolescent girls, women, pregnant women and new mothers need the best foods available: milk, fresh fruit and vegetables, meat, fish, eggs, grains, peas and beans. All of these foods are safe to eat during pregnancy and while breastfeeding.

Women will feel stronger and be healthier during pregnancy if they eat nutritious meals, consume greater quantities of nutritious food and get more rest than usual. Nutritious foods rich in iron, vitamin A and folic acid include meat, fish, eggs, green leafy vegetables, and orange or yellow fruits and vegetables.

After childbirth, women also need nutritious meals and a greater quantity of food and rest. Breastfeeding mothers need about 500 extra calories per day, the equivalent of an additional meal.

During prenatal visits, a trained health worker can provide the pregnant woman with iron-folic acid or multiple micronutrient supplements to prevent or treat anaemia. Malaria or hookworm infection can be treated if needed. The health worker can also screen the pregnant woman for night blindness and, as necessary, prescribe an adequate dosage of vitamin A to treat the woman and contribute to the healthy development of the fetus.

If the pregnant woman thinks she has anaemia, malaria or hookworms, she should consult a trained health worker.

Salt consumed by families should be iodized. Iodine in a pregnant woman's and young child's diet is especially critical for the healthy development of the child's brain. Goitre, a swelling at the front of the neck, is a clear sign that the body is not getting enough iodine. A diet low in iodine is especially damaging during the early stages of pregnancy and in early childhood. Women who do not have enough iodine in their diet are more likely to have an infant who is mentally or physically disabled. Severe iodine deficiency can cause cretinism (stunted physical and mental growth), stillbirth, miscarriage and increased risk of infant mortality.

KEY MESSAGE

3.

Every pregnancy is special. All pregnant women need at least four prenatal care visits to help ensure a safe and healthy pregnancy. Pregnant women and their families need to be able to recognize the signs of labour and the warning signs of pregnancy complications. They need to have plans and resources for obtaining skilled care for the birth and immediate help if problems arise.

SUPPORTING INFORMATION

When a young woman begins to be sexually active, she needs information about pregnancy and the risks of sexually transmitted infections (STIs), including HIV. She should be able to recognize the early signs of pregnancy. If she becomes pregnant, she should be supported to receive prenatal care early in the pregnancy from a trained health worker. She should learn about the normal phases of pregnancy and how to keep herself and her baby healthy during the pregnancy. She needs to know the warning signs of serious pregnancy complications.

A pregnant woman needs at least four prenatal visits with a trained health worker during every pregnancy. The first prenatal visit should take place as early as possible, ideally in the first three months (the first trimester) of pregnancy, and the other three visits can be scheduled to take place at predetermined times during the remainder of the pregnancy.

To help ensure a safe and healthy pregnancy, a trained health worker or skilled birth attendant should:

- provide the pregnant woman with information on the changes occurring in her body

- check for high blood pressure, which can be dangerous to both mother and child

- check for anaemia and provide iron-folic acid supplements, ensure that the woman understands the importance of taking the supplements and explain the normal side effects, including constipation and nausea

- screen for night blindness to determine if the woman needs to be treated with vitamin A and, if necessary, prescribe vitamin A to protect the mother and promote the healthy development of the fetus

- review the mother's tetanus immunization status and give the dose(s) needed to protect her and her newborn baby

- encourage all pregnant women to use only iodized salt in food preparation to help protect their children from mental and physical disabilities and to protect themselves from goitre

- encourage all pregnant women to have more nutritious meals, increased quantities of food and more rest than usual

- prescribe antimalarial tablets and recommend use of an insecticide-treated mosquito net where needed

- prescribe deworming medication, as necessary, from the second trimester onward to help reduce low birthweight

- prepare the mother and father for the experience of childbirth and caring for their newborn, give the mother advice on breastfeeding and caring for herself, and provide the father with guidance on how he can assist

- advise the pregnant woman and her family on where the birth should take place and how to get help if complications arise before and during childbirth or immediately after delivery

- provide referrals when needed to groups in the community that provide support and protect pregnant women living with violence

- advise on how to avoid STIs, including HIV

- check for infections during pregnancy, especially urinary tract infections and STIs, including HIV, and treat them with appropriate medications

- provide voluntary and confidential HIV testing and counselling.

A pregnant woman who is HIV-positive should consult a trained health worker for counselling on how to reduce the risk of infecting her baby during pregnancy, childbirth and breastfeeding and how to care for herself and her baby. A pregnant woman who thinks she may be infected with HIV should be supported to get tested and receive counselling. The father-to-be should also be tested and counselled (*refer to the HIV chapter for more information*).

Every pregnant woman and her family need to know that pregnancy and childbearing can have risks. They should be able to recognize the warning signs.

It is generally recommended that women give birth in a facility and with a skilled birth attendant, since complications cannot be predicted. For some women, this is even more important because the possibility of complications increases if they:

- are under 18 or over 35 years of age
- gave birth less than two years ago
- have had several previous pregnancies
- have had a previous premature birth or a baby weighing less than 2 kilograms at birth
- have had a previous difficult birth or Caesarean birth
- have had a miscarriage or stillbirth
- weigh less than 38 kilograms
- are less than 1.5 metres tall
- have been through infibulation or genital cutting
- have HIV or other STIs.

A pregnant woman should be supported to recognize the signs of labour and know when it is time to seek a skilled birth attendant to assist with the birth.

The signs of labour include any one of the following:

- painful contractions every 20 minutes or less
- the water breaks
- bloody, sticky discharge.

Warning signs during pregnancy include:

- anaemia (symptoms include paleness of the tongue and inside the eyelids, fatigue and shortness of breath)
- unusual swelling of legs, arms or face
- little or no movement of the fetus.

Signs that mean help is needed immediately include:

- spotting or bleeding from the vagina

- severe headaches, blurred vision

- convulsions (fits)

- severe abdominal pain

- fever and weakness

- fast or difficult breathing

- labour pains for more than 12 hours.

During the prenatal visits, the pregnant woman and her family should be supported in preparing for the birth and possible complications by developing a plan that specifies:

- where the woman will give birth and where she will go if complications arise

- who will accompany her

- how she will get there

- what supplies she needs to take for herself and her baby

- what costs are involved and how they will be covered

- who will help take care of her family while she is away

- who can donate blood if it is needed.

Because conditions may change, the plan for the birth and possible complications should be updated during every prenatal care visit as the pregnancy progresses.

The plan for emergency care in case of complications should include the location of the nearest maternity clinic or hospital and the resources needed to quickly get the woman there at any time of the day or night.

All pregnant women should have access to a maternity clinic or hospital when they give birth. This is particularly important if the woman and her family are aware that the birth is likely to be difficult. In some cases, where distance and/or an expected risky birth are factors, it may be preferable to have the mother-to-be move closer to the clinic or hospital as her due date approaches so she is within quick reach of health services.

Health workers, families and communities need to give special attention to pregnant adolescents because they are at higher risk of pregnancy complications and in some cases they may lack the influence to make family decisions or ask for assistance.

4.

Childbirth is the most critical period for the mother and her baby. Every pregnant woman must have a skilled birth attendant, such as a midwife, doctor or nurse, assisting her during childbirth, and she must also have timely access to specialized care if complications should occur.

SUPPORTING INFORMATION

Every pregnancy deserves attention because there is always a risk of something going wrong with the mother, baby or both. Many dangers, illnesses or even death can be avoided if the woman plans to give birth attended by a skilled birth attendant, such as a doctor, nurse or midwife, and makes at least four prenatal visits to a trained health worker during the pregnancy.

The likelihood of the mother or the baby becoming ill or dying is reduced when childbirth takes place in a properly equipped health facility with the assistance of a skilled birth attendant, who also checks regularly on the mother and baby in the 24 hours after delivery.

When the pregnant woman is ready to give birth, she should be encouraged to have a companion of her choice accompany her to provide her with continuous support during childbirth and after birth. In particular, the companion can support the woman in labour to eat and drink, use breathing techniques for different stages of childbirth, and arrange for pain and discomfort relief as needed and advised by the skilled birth attendant.

During and immediately following childbirth, the skilled birth attendant will:

- assess and follow the progress of labour and pay attention to danger signs that indicate help is needed *immediately*

- advise the woman and her family if specialized care is needed and if a transfer to a hospital or maternity centre is necessary

- reduce the risk of infection by keeping hands, instruments and the delivery area clean, and by using gloves at appropriate times

- encourage the woman to walk during the first stage of labour and support her choice of position for childbirth

- assist the different stages of labour and the birth of the baby

- cut the umbilical cord at the appropriate moment and care for it

- care for the baby and keep her or him warm after birth

- guide the mother to put her baby on her chest for immediate skin-to-skin contact and initiation of breastfeeding soon after birth

- deliver the afterbirth (placenta) safely and care for the mother after the baby is born

- examine and weigh the baby and put recommended drops in the baby's eyes to prevent blindness and infection

- manage newborn health problems and refer or transfer the baby with the mother to an appropriate health provider or health facility, if necessary.

5.

Post-natal care for the mother and child reduces the risk of complications and supports mothers and fathers or other caregivers to help their new baby get a healthy start in life. The mother and child should be checked regularly during the first 24 hours after childbirth, in the first week, and again six weeks after birth. If there are complications, more frequent check-ups are necessary.

SUPPORTING INFORMATION

Post-natal care assisted by a skilled birth attendant is important to help ensure the survival and health of the mother and her newborn. During the first hours after childbirth and the first week and month of life, newborn babies are *particularly* vulnerable.

After childbirth the skilled birth attendant will:

- check the mother's and baby's health regularly during the 24 hours after birth, during the first week, and again six weeks after birth

- advise and support the mother on how to continue breastfeeding the baby

- advise the new parents on how to prevent or delay another birth

- advise the mother on nutrition, rest, hygiene, immunizations, sleeping under an insecticide-treated mosquito net in malarial areas, regular health check-ups and how to care for herself and her baby; advise the father to be supportive of these needs of the mother and child

- explain potential danger signs for the mother and her baby

- support the mother, father and family in preparing an emergency plan in the event complications arise

- advise mothers and fathers on STIs, including HIV, and if they are infected with HIV, how to care for themselves and their child and how to practise breastfeeding in a way that reduces the risk of infecting the child

- counsel the mother who is HIV-positive and her partner to help them make informed decisions on future pregnancies and contraceptive methods (*refer to the HIV chapter for more information*)

- schedule the next follow-up visit for the mother and her baby.

For the mother and/or child with complications, the skilled birth attendant will:

- explain to the mother any complications she or her baby had and the treatment received and how she should continue to care for herself and her baby at home

- provide the mother with medications if necessary and instructions on how, when, and for how long to administer them

- identify and administer missing immunizations to the mother, including tetanus toxoid

- advise the mother and father or other caregivers on how to best care for their baby if born too soon or too small, or with other special needs

- schedule frequent follow-up visits to assess the health of the mother and her baby.

The first days and weeks are especially risky for low-birthweight babies. The majority of newborn deaths occur in low-birthweight babies. Many of these babies could be saved with post-natal care provided by a skilled birth attendant who will:

- identify and address the danger signs in a timely manner

- provide extra support for breastfeeding, including expressing milk and cup feeding

- ensure the baby is warm by helping the mother or other caregiver use skin-to-skin care, also known as the 'Kangaroo Mother Care' method

- refer the baby for emergency care if the infant is unable to breastfeed or accept expressed milk.

KEY MESSAGE

6.

A healthy mother, a safe birth, essential newborn care and attention, a loving family and a clean home environment contribute greatly to newborn health and survival.

SUPPORTING INFORMATION

Newborns need to be carefully cared for around the clock, loved, kept clean and warm, and fed. Mothers and fathers or other primary caregivers who meet their basic needs contribute to building the foundation of the babies' future health, happiness, growth, learning and development.

A newborn thrives when she or he is:

- kept close to and frequently held and cuddled by the mother, father or other primary caregiver

- exclusively breastfed from birth through the first six months on demand and at least eight times in a 24-hour period, contributing to bonding between the infant and the mother and giving the baby immunity against infections

- loved and given affection, attention, encouragement and stimulation from her or his family members, helping the baby to grow and learn rapidly

- kept warm, clean, comfortable and safe, and changed regularly and burped after feeding

- cared for in a clean environment that helps to prevent infections

- provided with quality health care, including regular check-ups with timely immunizations and weighing to monitor growth.

A skilled birth attendant will:

- respond to new parents' questions on caring for their newborn that may relate to breastfeeding, formula feeding, immunizations, bathing the baby, interacting with the baby, language development, sleeping patterns and more

- inform the new parents of danger signs in an infant that require immediate medical attention

- help mothers and fathers develop their emergency plan in case complications should arise with their baby

- provide the mother and father with a record of essential information about the baby at birth (weight, height, time of birth)

- issue the baby's birth certificate for parents to report the birth to the civil registrar.

Babies born early or with low birthweight or babies with other special needs require special care, love and attention to ensure their survival and optimal growth and development.

A skilled birth attendant can play a critical role in instructing the mother and father on how to care for their baby with special needs.

Some babies may need extra care at a special care unit of a hospital until they are sufficiently developed or well enough to go home with the parents. If a baby is not yet able to breastfeed, the mother can express her milk and safely store it so it can be fed to the baby using a sterilized feeding tube, spoon or cup.

Caring for a newborn brings joy to the mother and father as well as anxiety and fatigue as they adjust to having full-time care of the new baby in their lives. Since newborns are generally dependent on their parents to provide for their every need, mothers and fathers need to take good care of themselves. Breastfeeding mothers especially need to eat more nutritious food, and all mothers should get more rest. A father can support the mother while she breastfeeds by caring for the household and other children or by caring for the newborn while she rests.

7.

Smoking, alcohol, drugs, poisons and pollutants are particularly harmful to pregnant women, the developing fetus, babies and young children.

SUPPORTING INFORMATION

If a pregnant woman smokes, her child is more likely to be born underweight. Her child is also more likely to have coughs, colds, croup, pneumonia or other breathing problems.

A pregnant woman can damage her own health and the health of the fetus by drinking alcohol or using narcotics. These substances can severely affect a child's physical and mental development. The mother-to-be should stop drinking alcohol and/or taking drugs as soon as she plans a pregnancy or suspects she is pregnant. If she has difficulty stopping, she should seek medical advice and support from a trained health worker, a health centre or a substance-abuse organization.

A pregnant woman should not take medicines during pregnancy unless they are absolutely necessary and prescribed by a trained health worker.

To ensure proper physical growth and mental development of the child, women of childbearing age, pregnant women, mothers and young children need to be protected from smoke from tobacco or cooking fires; from pesticides, herbicides and other poisons; and from pollutants such as lead found in water transported by lead pipes, in vehicle exhaust and in some paints.

Families and communities can especially help pregnant women, mothers and their children by supporting smoke-free environments so they do not inhale damaging secondary tobacco smoke.

Workplaces should protect women of childbearing age, pregnant women and mothers from exposure to harmful smoke, poisons and pollutants that can affect their health and that of their children.

8.

Violence against women is a serious public health problem in most communities. When a woman is pregnant, violence is very dangerous to both the woman and her pregnancy. It increases the risk of miscarriage, premature labour and having a low-birthweight baby.

SUPPORTING INFORMATION

Violence and abuse are unacceptable at any time. Women who are abused during pregnancy may suffer from early labour and could lose their babies as a result. Babies can be born with low birthweight, which can affect their health and survival.

Health workers, families and communities should be aware of these dangers, provide protection, and work to prevent and eliminate violence against women. Local authorities, with support from organizations and community leaders, have the responsibility to: (1) take action to prevent violence against women and challenge social norms that increase women's risk for violence and abuse; (2) enforce laws protecting women from violence and abuse; and (3) provide accessible protection and support services for abused women.

9.

In the workplace, pregnant women and mothers should be protected from discrimination and exposure to health risks and granted time to breastfeed or express breastmilk. They should be entitled to maternity leave, employment protection, medical benefits and, where applicable, cash support.

SUPPORTING INFORMATION

Worldwide, nearly 60 per cent of women of childbearing age were in the labour force as of 2006. Many women work in the informal economy, where their work is not recorded, regulated or protected by public authorities. Whether women work in the formal or informal economy, it is important that protective measures are put in place in communities, with support from the government and civil society, to safeguard the health and economic security of women, children and families.

Protective measures can include:

Maternity leave: A mother has the right to a period of rest when her child is born, means to support herself and her family, and a guarantee that she can return to work when her leave is finished.

Employment protection: This is a guarantee that pregnant women and new mothers will not be discriminated against and lose their job or job entitlements (pension, paid holiday leave, etc.) due to pregnancy, maternity leave or time off for childbirth

Cash (income) support and medical benefits: Working pregnant women and mothers and their newborns and families generally need cash support and medical care benefits. Cash support replaces a portion of lost income caused by the interruption of the women's work due to pregnancy, childbirth and newborn care. Medical benefits are needed by pregnant women, new mothers and newborns for prenatal, childbirth and post-natal services, and hospitalization when necessary.

Health protection: The pregnant or nursing woman should not be obliged to perform work that can affect her health or that of her child. Where there is a risk, changes in her work conditions should be made to reduce workplace health risks. The woman should return to her job when it is safe for her to do so, or she should be provided with an equivalent job with the same remuneration.

Breastfeeding: Mothers should have the right to breastfeed a child after returning to work, because breastfeeding has major benefits for the health of the mother and her child. Mothers should be entitled to take one or more breaks, or a reduction in work hours for breastfeeding, which should not be subtracted from her paid work time.

KEY MESSAGE

10.

Every woman has the right to quality health care, especially a pregnant woman or a new mother. Health workers should be technically competent and sensitive to cultural practices and should treat all women, including adolescent girls, with respect.

SUPPORTING INFORMATION

Many dangers of pregnancy and childbirth can be avoided if women have access to quality health care during pregnancy and childbirth and after childbirth.

All women have the right to the services of a skilled birth attendant, such as a doctor, nurse or midwife, and to emergency care if complications should arise.

Quality health care that offers information and counselling enables women and men to make informed decisions about their reproductive health. A woman in need of maternal care should be supported by her husband or partner and family to take good care of herself and her baby and to reach a health facility when needed, including for prenatal care, childbirth, post-natal care and emergency care.

Governments, with support from communities, should make sure that the cost of health services does not prevent women, including adolescent girls, from using them. Other barriers such as the cost of transport, long distances, difficult roads and cultural practices also need to be addressed to ensure access to health services.

Health-care providers should be supported through regular training to maintain and improve their technical and communication skills needed to provide quality health care. They should be trained to treat all women with respect, to be sensitive to cultural norms and practices, and to respect a person's right to confidentiality and privacy. They need to be sensitive and understanding of the particular needs of adolescents, and know how to support and counsel them in caring for themselves and their babies.

Why it is important to share and act on information about

CHILD DEVELOPMENT AND EARLY LEARNING

Child development refers to the changes that occur as a child grows and develops in relation to being physically healthy, mentally alert, emotionally sound, socially competent and ready to learn.

The first five years of a child's life are fundamentally important. They are the foundation that shapes children's future health, happiness, growth, development and learning achievement at school, in the family and community, and in life in general.

Recent research confirms that the first five years are particularly important for the development of the child's brain, and the first three years are the most critical in shaping the child's brain architecture. Early experiences provide the base for the brain's organizational development and functioning throughout life. They have a direct impact on how children develop learning skills as well as social and emotional abilities.

Children learn more quickly during their early years than at any other time in life. They need love and nurturing to develop a sense of trust and security that turns into confidence as they grow.

Babies and young children grow, learn and develop rapidly when they receive love and affection, attention, encouragement and mental stimulation, as well as nutritious meals and good health care.

Understanding the stages of child development helps parents know what to expect and how to best support the child as she or he grows and develops.

In many settings, early childhood programmes support parents and their children from infancy through age 8, which includes the important transition from home to school.

All children have the right to be raised in a family and to have access to quality health care, good nutrition, education, play and protection from harm, abuse and discrimination. Children have the right to grow up in an environment in which they are enabled to reach their full potential in life.

It is the duty of parents, other caregivers and family members, communities, civil society and governments to ensure that these rights are respected, protected and fulfilled.

KEY MESSAGES:
What every family and community
has a right to know about

CHILD DEVELOPMENT AND EARLY LEARNING

1. The early years, especially the first three years of life, are very important for building the baby's brain. Everything she or he sees, touches, tastes, smells or hears helps to shape the brain for thinking, feeling, moving and learning.

2. Babies learn rapidly from the moment of birth. They grow and learn best when responsive and caring parents and other caregivers give them affection, attention and stimulation in addition to good nutrition, proper health care and protection.

3. Encouraging children to play and explore helps them learn and develop socially, emotionally, physically and intellectually. This helps children get ready for school.

4. Children learn how to behave (socially and emotionally) by imitating the behaviour of those closest to them.

5. Entering primary school on time is critical to ensure the continuity of a child's development. Support from parents, other caregivers, teachers and the community is very important.

6. All children grow and develop in similar patterns, but each child develops at her or his own pace. Every child has her or his own interests, temperament, style of social interaction and approach to learning.

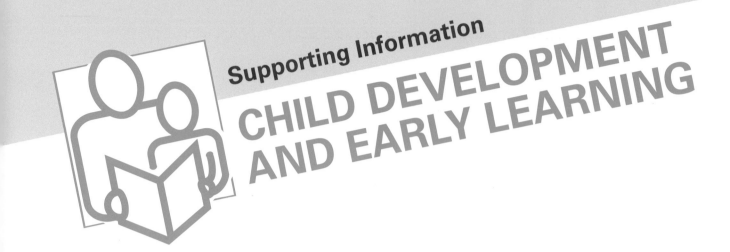

CHILD DEVELOPMENT AND EARLY LEARNING

1.

The early years, especially the first three years of life, are very important for building the baby's brain. Everything she or he sees, touches, tastes, smells or hears helps to shape the brain for thinking, feeling, moving and learning.

SUPPORTING INFORMATION

A child's brain develops rapidly during the first five years of life, especially the first three years. It is a time of rapid cognitive, linguistic, social, emotional and motor development. For example, a child learns many words starting at around 15–18 months. Rapid language learning continues into the preschool years.

The child's brain grows as she or he sees, feels, tastes, smells and hears. Each time the child uses one of the senses, a neural connection is made in the child's brain. New experiences repeated many times help make new connections, which shape the way the child thinks, feels, behaves and learns now and in the future.

A close relationship between the child and the caregiver is the best way to nourish the child's growing brain. When a caregiver plays with and sings, speaks, reads or tells a story to the child and nurtures her or him with healthy food, love and affection, the child's brain grows. Being healthy, interacting with caregivers and living in a safe and clean environment can make a big difference in a child's growth, development and future potential.

Babies need lots of care and affection in the early years. Holding, cuddling and talking to the child stimulate brain growth and promote emotional development. Being kept close to the mother and breastfed on demand provide the infant with a sense of emotional security. The baby suckles for both nutrition and comfort.

For young children, crying is a way of communicating. Responding to the child's cry by holding and/or talking soothingly to her or him will help establish a sense of trust and security.

This kind of early bonding and attachment to the mother, father or other close caregiver helps a child develop a broad range of abilities to use and build upon throughout life. These include the ability to:

- learn

- be self-confident and have high self-esteem

- have positive social skills

- have successful relationships at later ages

- develop a sense of empathy.

As children's brains develop, so do their emotions, which are real and powerful. Children may become frustrated if they are unable to do something or have something they want. They are often frightened of strangers, new situations or the dark. Children whose reactions are laughed at, punished or ignored may grow up shy and unable to express emotions normally. If caregivers are patient and sympathetic when a child expresses strong emotions, the child is more likely to grow up happy, secure and well balanced.

Boys and girls have the same physical, mental, emotional and social needs. Both have the same capacity for learning. Both have the same need for affection, attention and approval.

Young children can experience excessive stress if they are physically or emotionally punished, are exposed to violence, are neglected or abused, or live in families with mental illness, such as depression or substance abuse. These stresses interfere with the developing brain and can lead to cognitive, social and emotional delays and behaviour problems in childhood and later in life.

Children who are physically or mentally punished in anger are more likely to become violent themselves. More positive and effective ways to address children's behaviour can include:

- providing a child with clear explanations about what to do and what not to do

- responding consistently to certain behaviours

- praising good behaviour.

These responses by parents and other caregivers encourage children so they become well-adjusted and productive members of the family and community.

Both parents, as well as other family members, need to be involved in caring and nurturing the growth, learning and development of children. They should make both girls and boys feel equally valued as they encourage them to learn and explore – this is important preparation for school.

Mothers around the world generally take on the primary role of addressing their children's rights and needs. They love, feed, console, teach, play with and care for their children.

A father's role is as vital as the mother's in nurturing and caring for their children and protecting their rights. A father should make daughters and sons feel they are equally important. Just like the mother, the father can help meet their child's needs for love, affection, approval, encouragement and stimulation. Together, the mother and father can ensure that the child receives a quality education and good nutrition and health care.

2.

Babies learn rapidly from the moment of birth. They grow and learn best when responsive and caring parents and other caregivers give them affection, attention and stimulation in addition to good nutrition, proper health care and protection.

SUPPORTING INFORMATION

Touch, hearing, smell, sight and taste are learning tools the child uses to explore and understand her or his world.

Affection, attention and stimulation

Children's minds develop rapidly when they are talked to, touched and cuddled; when they see and hear familiar faces and voices; and when they handle different objects.

Children learn quickly when they feel loved and secure from birth and when they play and interact with family members and other people close to them. The more often mothers, fathers and other caregivers play with, talk to and respond to the child, the faster she or he learns.

Parents and other caregivers should consistently talk, read and sing to infants and young children. Even if the child is not yet able to understand the words, these early 'conversations' help to develop social and language skills and learning capacities.

Parents and other caregivers can help children learn and grow by giving them new, interesting and safe things to look at, listen to, smell, hold and play with.

Children who feel secure and loved usually do better in school, are more self-confident, have good self-esteem and are able to cope more easily with life's challenges.

Good nutrition

Exclusive breastfeeding on demand for the first six months, timely introduction of safe and nutritious foods at the age of 6 months and continued breastfeeding for two years or beyond provide the child with optimal nutrition and health benefits. Feeding time is also an opportunity for the child to receive affection and have contact with the mother, father or other caregiver.

Good nutrition is vital for a child's growth and development. The diet of a pregnant woman and that of a young child should be varied and nutritious. It should include essential nutrients such as proteins and essential fats to help a child's body grow and have energy, vitamin A to help a child resist illness, iodine to help ensure the healthy development of a child's brain, and iron to protect a child's mental and physical abilities.

While the mother has the primary role of breastfeeding the child, the father can support her by making sure she has nutritious food, helping with household and childcare responsibilities, and being emotionally supportive of her, the baby, the older children and other family members.

Proper health care

The health worker should inform parents and other caregivers about:

- necessary immunizations and the schedule to follow
- how to avoid anaemia and parasitic diseases in children over 6 months of age
- why deworming is important
- how to ensure that the child gets enough nutrients, such as iron and vitamin A, for her or his healthy mental and physical development.

Children who are anaemic, malnourished or frequently sick may become fearful and upset more easily than healthy children. They will also lack the drive to play, explore and interact with others. These children need special attention, care and encouragement to eat, play and interact with others in order to become healthy.

Infants who have completed their immunizations on time and are receiving proper nutrition, health care, love and affection have an increased chance of survival. They are able to concentrate on exploring, learning and developing cognitive, language, social, emotional and motor skills.

Protection and care from responsive and caring parents and/or other caregivers

Babies and small children should not be left alone for long periods of time. This delays their physical and mental development. It also puts them at risk of accidents.

Girls need the same amount of food, attention, affection and care that boys need. All babies and young children need to be encouraged and praised when they learn to do something new and say new words.

All girls and boys should have their birth registered in order to help ensure their right to access basic services, such as health care, education and legal and social services.

3.

Encouraging children to play and explore helps them learn and develop socially, emotionally, physically and intellectually. This helps children get ready for school.

SUPPORTING INFORMATION

Children play because it is fun. Play is also key to their learning and development. Playing, both structured and unstructured, lays the foundation for a child's development of future learning and life skills. It helps children:

- develop their knowledge, experience, curiosity and confidence
- learn by trying things, comparing results, asking questions and meeting challenges
- develop the skills of language, thinking, planning, organizing and decision-making.

Stimulation, play and being included in play with other children and adults are very important for children with disabilities or chronic illnesses, such as children with HIV.

When parents and other caregivers talk and interact with children in their first language, it helps children develop the ability to think and express themselves. Children learn language quickly and easily through hearing and singing songs, having stories told or read to them, repeating rhymes and playing games.

Girls and boys need the same opportunities for play and interaction with all family members, including siblings and grandparents, and in activities outside the home. Play and interaction with the mother and the father help strengthen the bond between the child and both parents.

Family members and other caregivers can help children learn by giving them simple tasks with clear instructions, providing objects to play with and suggesting new activities. They should not dominate the child's play.

All children need a variety of simple play materials that are suitable for their stage of development and learning. Water, sand, cardboard boxes, wooden building blocks, and pots and lids are just as good for facilitating a child's play and learning as toys bought from a shop.

Parents and caregivers need to be patient when a very young child insists on trying to do something without help. Children learn by trying until they succeed. As long as the child is protected from danger, struggling to do something new and difficult is a positive step in the child's development.

Children are constantly changing and developing new abilities. Caregivers should notice these changes and follow the child's lead. Responding to and encouraging children helps them develop more quickly.

As young children grow older they need opportunities to learn and socialize with other children of their age. Group learning activities, run by a trained caregiver or teacher at home or in a nursery school or kindergarten, are important in helping children get ready for school.

KEY MESSAGE

4. Children learn how to behave (socially and emotionally) by imitating the behaviour of those closest to them.

SUPPORTING INFORMATION

By watching and imitating others, young children learn how to interact socially. They learn acceptable and unacceptable kinds of behaviour.

The examples set by adults, older siblings and children are the most powerful influences shaping a child's behaviour and personality. One way children learn is by copying what others do. If men and women do not treat each other equally, the child will observe, learn and probably copy this behaviour. If adults shout, behave violently, exclude or discriminate, children will learn this type of behaviour. If adults treat others with kindness, respect and patience, children will follow their example. If mothers and fathers treat each other with love and respect, this is what their children will learn and most likely 'replay' in their adult relationships.

Children like to pretend. This should be encouraged, as it develops their imagination and creativity. It also helps the child understand different ways people behave.

5.

Entering primary school on time is critical to ensure the continuity of a child's development. Support from parents, other caregivers, teachers and the community is very important.

SUPPORTING INFORMATION

In most countries, children start primary school at around 6 or 7 years of age. Starting school is a critical stage in a child's development.

Both girls and boys should start school at the appropriate age (in accordance with their country's policy). By the time they enter school, they should have basic cognitive and language skills and sufficient social competency and emotional development to allow them to enjoy learning in the formal school setting.

The support of parents and other caregivers is very important for children's successful transition to school. Parents and other caregivers should equally and fully support both girls and boys in attending school regularly and being well prepared. They should also be involved in school activities. This helps children adapt to the school setting, settle more quickly into the school learning environment and attend school regularly.

Teachers should be prepared to support young children who are still developing their basic potential for learning. Teachers have a key role in building the confidence of both girls and boys so that they can equally enjoy and succeed at learning. Play continues to be a basic medium of teaching and learning in the early school years. A child-friendly school that supports active learning and promotes participation offers the best learning environment for children.

Along with families and the school, the community – both local authorities and civil society – can contribute to:

- making school a priority within the community

- making sure the school is a safe and welcoming place for all children

- making sure the school has the resources it needs, including community members involved in school management and parent-teacher associations.

6.

All children grow and develop in similar patterns, but each child develops at her or his own pace. Every child has her or his own interests, temperament, style of social interaction and approach to learning.

Understanding the ages and stages of child development helps parents understand the changes to expect as a child grows and develops (*refer to the the following chart*). Parents or other caregivers should be able to seek help when they feel their child is not developing as expected.

By observing how young children respond to touch, sound and sight, parents can identify signs of possible developmental problems or disabilities. If a young child is developing slowly, parents and other caregivers can help by spending extra time with the child, playing and talking with the child, and massaging the child's body.

If the child does not respond to attention and stimulation, parents and other caregivers need to seek help from a trained health worker. Taking early action is very important in helping children who have delays and disabilities reach their full potential. Parents and other caregivers need to encourage the greatest possible development of the child's abilities.

A girl or boy with a disability needs lots of love and extra protection. She or he needs all the same attention, care and support every other child needs: birth registration, breastfeeding, immunizations, nutritious food, and protection from abuse and violence. Like all children, children with disabilities should be encouraged to play and interact with other children.

A child who is unhappy or experiencing emotional difficulties may exhibit unusual behaviour. Examples include:

- suddenly becoming emotional, unfriendly, sad, lazy or unhelpful
- consistently acting out or misbehaving
- crying often
- having sleep difficulties
- becoming violent with other children
- sitting alone instead of playing with family or friends
- suddenly having no interest in usual activities or schoolwork
- losing appetite.

The child's parents or other caregivers should be encouraged to talk with and listen to the child. If the problem persists, they should seek help from a trained health worker or teacher.

If a child has mental or emotional difficulties or has been abused, she or he needs mental health or counselling services. The child should be assessed to determine what support and treatment are needed.

The following chart gives parents an idea of how young children develop. Each stage of development is part of a continuum, building on the previous stage and affecting the next. Not all children grow and develop at the same pace. Slow progress may be normal or may be due to inadequate nutrition, poor health, lack of stimulation or a more serious problem. Parents may wish to discuss their child's progress with a trained health worker or a teacher.

HOW CHILDREN DEVELOP

By the age of 1 MONTH

A baby should be able to:	
	• turn her or his head towards a hand that is stroking the child's cheek or mouth
	• bring both hands towards her or his mouth
	• turn towards familiar voices and sounds
	• suckle the breast and touch it with her or his hands.

Advice for parents and other caregivers:	
	• make skin-to-skin contact and breastfeed within one hour of birth
	• support the baby's head when you hold the baby upright
	• massage and cuddle the baby often
	• always handle the baby gently, even when you are tired or upset
	• breastfeed frequently and on demand
	• always safely dispose of the baby's faeces and wash hands with soap and water or a substitute, such as ash and water, after changing the baby
	• talk, read and sing to the child as much as possible
	• give consistent love and affection
	• visit a trained health worker with the infant during the first week and again six weeks after birth.

Warning signs to watch for:	• poor suckling at the breast or refusing to suckle
	• little movement of arms and legs
	• little or no reaction to loud sounds or bright lights
	• crying for long periods for no apparent reason
	• vomiting and diarrhoea, which can lead to dehydration.

By the age of **6 MONTHS**

A baby should be able to:	• raise the head and chest when lying on her or his stomach
	• reach for dangling objects
	• grasp and shake objects
	• roll both ways
	• sit with support
	• explore objects with hands and mouth
	• begin to imitate sounds and facial expressions
	• respond to her or his own name and to familiar faces.
Advice for parents and other caregivers:	• lay the baby on a clean, flat, safe surface so she or he can move freely and reach for objects
	• continue to hold and cuddle the baby every day, giving consistent love and affection
	• prop or hold the baby in a secure position so she or he can see what is happening nearby
	• continue to breastfeed on demand day and night, and start adding other foods (two to three meals a day starting at 6 months; three to four meals a day from 9 months)
	• talk, read or sing to the child as often as possible, not only when she or he is hungry or getting ready to sleep.
Warning signs to watch for:	• stiffness or difficulty moving limbs
	• constant moving of the head (this might indicate an ear infection, which could lead to deafness if not treated)
	• little or no response to sounds, familiar faces or the breast
	• refusing the breast or other foods.

CHILD DEVELOPMENT AND EARLY LEARNING

A baby should be able to:	
	sit without support
	crawl on hands and knees and pull herself or himself up to stand
	take steps holding on to support
	try to imitate words and sounds and respond to simple requests
	enjoy playing and clapping
	repeat sounds and gestures for attention
	pick things up with thumb and one finger
	start holding objects such as a spoon and cup and attempt self-feeding.

Advice for parents and other caregivers:	
	point to objects and name them; play with, talk, sing and read to the child frequently
	use mealtimes and other family activities to encourage interaction with all family members
	give consistent affection and be responsive both when the child is happy and when upset
	if the child is developing slowly or has a physical disability, focus on the child's abilities and give extra stimulation and interaction
	do not leave a child in one position for many hours
	make the area as safe as possible to prevent accidents, and keep dangerous objects, such as sharp objects, plastic bags and small items a child can choke on, out of the child's reach
	continue to breastfeed and ensure that the child has enough food and a variety of family foods
	help the child experiment with spoon and cup feeding
	make sure the child's immunizations are up to date and that she or he receives all recommended doses of nutrient supplements
	keep the child's hands clean and begin teaching the child to wash them with soap.

Warning signs to watch for:	
	does not make sounds in response to others
	does not look at objects that move
	listlessness and lack of response to the caregiver
	lack of appetite or refusal of food.

A child should be able to	
	walk, climb and run
	point to objects or pictures when they are named (e.g., nose, eyes, ears)
	say several words together (from about 15 months)
	follow simple instructions
	scribble if given a pencil or crayon
	enjoy simple stories and songs
	imitate the behaviour of others
	begin to eat by herself or himself.

Advice for parents and other caregivers:	• read to and sing or play games with the child
	• teach the child to avoid dangerous objects
	• talk to the child normally – do not use baby talk
	• continue to breastfeed and ensure the child has enough food and a variety of family foods
	• make sure the child is fully immunized
	• encourage, but do not force, the child to eat
	• provide simple rules and set reasonable expectations
	• praise the child's achievements, provide reassurance when the child is afraid and continue to give consistent affection every day.
Warning signs to watch for:	• lack of response to others
	• difficulty keeping balance while walking
	• injuries and unexplained changes in behaviour (especially if the child has been cared for by others)
	• lack of appetite.

By the age of 3 YEARS

A child should be able to:	• walk, run, climb, kick and jump easily
	• recognize and identify common objects and pictures by pointing
	• make sentences of two or three words
	• say her or his own name and age
	• name colours
	• understand numbers
	• use make-believe objects in play
	• feed herself or himself
	• express affection.
Advice for parents and other caregivers:	• read and look at books with the child and talk about the pictures
	• tell the child stories and teach rhymes and songs
	• give the child her or his own bowl or plate of food
	• continue to encourage the child to eat, giving the child as much time as she or he needs
	• help the child learn to dress, use the toilet or latrine and wash her or his hands with soap and water or a substitute, such as ash and water, after defecating and before touching food and eating
	• listen to and answer all the child's questions
	• encourage creative play, building and drawing
	• give the child simple tasks, such as putting toys back in their place, to build responsibility
	• limit television watching and ensure that violent shows are not viewed
	• acknowledge and encourage positive behaviour and set clear limits
	• provide consistent affection every day
	• if available, enrol the child in an early learning (play) activity with other children.

CHILD DEVELOPMENT AND EARLY LEARNING

Warning signs to watch for:	<ul><li>loss of interest in playing</li><li>frequent falling</li><li>difficulty manipulating small objects</li><li>failure to understand simple messages</li><li>inability to speak using several words</li><li>little or no interest in food.</li></ul>

A child should be able to:	<ul><li>move in a coordinated way</li><li>speak in sentences and use many different words</li><li>understand opposites (e.g., fat and thin, tall and short)</li><li>play with other children</li><li>dress without help</li><li>answer simple questions</li><li>count 5–10 objects</li><li>wash her or his own hands.</li></ul>
Advice for parents and other caregivers:	<ul><li>listen to the child</li><li>interact frequently with the child</li><li>read and tell stories</li><li>encourage the child (both girls and boys) to play and explore</li><li>listen to and answer all the child's questions, have conversations (with both girls and boys)</li><li>encourage creative play, building and drawing</li><li>limit television watching and ensure that violent shows are not viewed</li><li>acknowledge and encourage positive behaviour and set clear and consistent limits</li><li>provide consistent affection every day</li><li>enrol the child (both girls and boys) in an early learning (play) programme that helps to prepare the child for school.</li></ul>
Warning signs to watch for:	<ul><li>fear, anger or violence when playing with other children, which could be signs of emotional problems or abuse.</li></ul>

A child's:	
	• physical development proceeds more gradually and steadily than in the early years
	• muscle mass increases, and small and large motor skills improve
	• ability to understand and communicate abstract concepts and complex ideas has begun to develop
	• span of attention increases, and she or he can focus on the past and future as well as the present
	• learning capacity is expanding, and she or he is learning to read, write and do problem solving in a school environment
	• friends and interactions with her or his peer group are increasingly important
	• interest in friendships includes enjoying time with her or his peer group and turning to peers for information
	• self-control improves, and understanding of more complex emotions increases.

Advice for parents and other caregivers:	
	• be a good role model, equally for girls and boys
	• encourage your child to express feelings and beliefs and to solve problems
	• recognize and support your child's strengths and skills as well as limitations
	• spend time with your child, and talk and listen to her or him
	• find activities you can do together that will make your child feel successful, secure and loved
	• facilitate and support your child's playtime with friends and in extra-curricular school activities
	• acknowledge and encourage positive behaviour and set clear and consistent limits
	• show interest and become involved in your child's school – remember that the mother, father and/or other caregiver(s) are a child's first and most important teachers.

Warning signs to watch for:	
	• difficulties making and keeping friends and participating in group activities
	• avoiding a task or challenge without trying, or showing signs of helplessness
	• trouble communicating needs, thoughts and emotions
	• trouble focusing on tasks, understanding and completing schoolwork
	• excessive aggression or shyness with friends and family.

CHILD DEVELOPMENT AND EARLY LEARNING

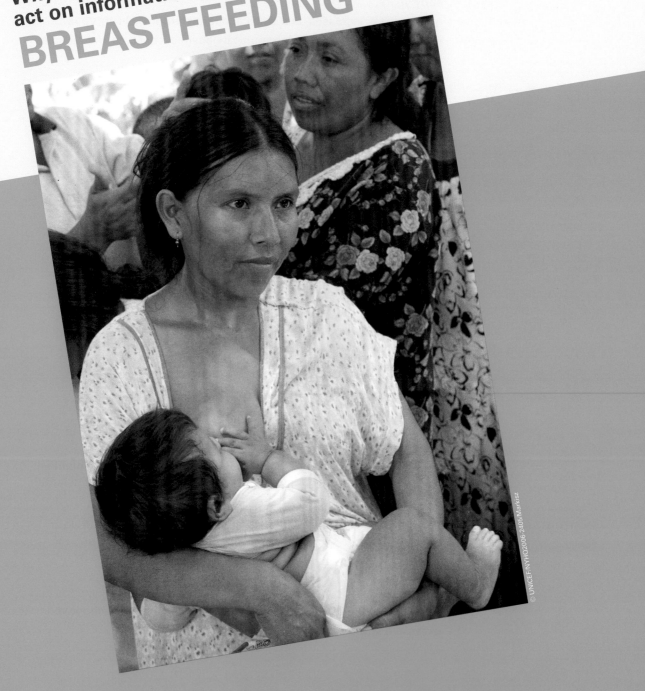

Why it is important to share and act on information about
BREASTFEEDING

Babies who are breastfed are generally healthier and achieve optimal growth and development compared to those who are fed formula milk.

If the vast majority of babies were exclusively fed breastmilk in their first six months of life – meaning *only* breastmilk and no other liquids or solids, not even water – it is estimated that the lives of at least 1.2 million children would be saved every year. If children continue to be breastfed up to two years and beyond, the health and development of millions of children would be greatly improved.

Infants who are not breastfed are at an increased risk of illness that can compromise their growth and raise the risk of death or disability. Breastfed babies receive protection from illnesses through the mother's milk.

Breastfeeding is the natural and recommended way of feeding all infants, even when artificial feeding is affordable, clean water is available, and good hygienic conditions for preparing and feeding infant formula exist.

If a mother is HIV-positive, there is a risk that she can transmit HIV to her baby through breastfeeding. Counselling can help her carefully weigh the risks and make an informed decision on which feeding option is best for her baby and most manageable for her.

Almost every mother can breastfeed successfully. All mothers, particularly those who might lack the confidence to breastfeed, need the encouragement and practical support of the baby's father and their families, friends and relatives. Health workers, community workers, women's organizations and employers can also provide support.

Everyone has the right to information about the benefits of breastfeeding and the risks of artificial feeding. Governments have a responsibility to provide this information. Communities as well as media and other channels of communication can play a key role in promoting breastfeeding.

KEY MESSAGES:
What every family and community has a right to know about
BREASTFEEDING

1. Breastmilk *alone* is the best food and drink for an infant for the first six months of life. No other food or drink, not even water, is usually needed during this period.

2. Newborn babies should be given to the mother to hold immediately after delivery. They should have skin-to-skin contact with the mother and begin breastfeeding within one hour of birth.

3. Almost every mother can breastfeed successfully. Breastfeeding the baby frequently causes production of more milk. The baby should breastfeed at least eight times daily, day and night, and on demand.

4. Breastfeeding helps protect babies and young children against dangerous illnesses. It also creates a special bond between mother and child.

5. Bottle feeding and giving a baby breastmilk substitutes such as infant formula or animal milk can threaten the baby's health and survival. If a woman cannot breastfeed her infant, the baby can be fed expressed breastmilk or, if necessary, a quality breastmilk substitute from an ordinary clean cup.

6. If a woman is infected with HIV, there is a risk that she can pass the infection to her infant through breastfeeding. In the first six months, this risk is much greater if the infant is fed both breastmilk and other liquids and foods than if fed breastmilk *alone*. Therefore, it is recommended that the baby receives breastmilk *alone* for the first six months, unless it is acceptable, feasible, affordable, sustainable and safe to give breastmilk substitutes (infant formula) exclusively.

7. A woman employed away from her home can continue to breastfeed her child. She should breastfeed as often as possible when she is with the infant and express her breastmilk when they are apart so that another caregiver can feed it to the baby in a clean and safe way.

8. After 6 months of age, when babies begin to eat foods, breastfeeding should continue for up to two years and beyond because it is an important source of nutrition, energy and protection from illness.

KEY MESSAGE

1. Breastmilk *alone* is the best food and drink for an infant for the first six months of life. No other food or drink, not even water, is usually needed during this period.

SUPPORTING INFORMATION

Breastmilk is the best food a young child can have. It promotes optimal growth and development and protects against illness. Breastmilk contains the perfect balance of nutrients for a baby, unlike infant formula, powdered milk or animal milk.

The baby does not need water or other drinks or foods (such as tea, juice, sugar water, gripe water, rice water, other milks, formula or porridge) during the first six months. Even in hot, dry climates, breastmilk fully meets a baby's need for fluids.

Breastmilk is easy for the baby to digest. A baby has difficulty digesting animal milks, and formula is digested much more slowly than breastmilk. Compared to other options, breastmilk nourishes the baby more efficiently.

Breastmilk protects against illness because it contains antibodies that transfer the mother's immunity or resistance to disease to the child. No other milks contain these antibodies.

Giving a baby under 6 months of age any liquids or foods other than breastmilk increases the risk of diarrhoea and other illnesses. Water and other liquids or foods may be contaminated, which can cause diarrhoea.

A baby who takes water or other liquids or foods in the first six months suckles less on the breast. This slows down breastmilk production.

If regular weighing shows that a breastfed baby under 6 months of age is not growing well:

- The mother may need help to improve the way the baby takes the breast into the mouth to ensure good attachment so the baby can suckle effectively.

- The baby may need more opportunities to breastfeed. The baby should breastfeed on demand, day and night, *at least* eight times during a 24-hour period. The baby should be allowed to breastfeed until she or he releases the breast and looks satisfied and sleepy. This shows that the baby has had all she or he wants from that breast. The baby should then be offered the other breast and may or may not want it. The baby should be kept on the breast until she or he has finished suckling.

- A low-birthweight baby may need frequent pauses during breastfeeding.

- The baby may be ill and should be checked by a trained health worker.

- The baby may be getting water or other fluids, which can reduce the intake of breastmilk. The mother may need guidance on how to reduce and eliminate other fluids and to increase and give only breastmilk.

Feeding a baby *only* with breastmilk and on demand during the first six months can help to delay the return of the mother's menstruation. This may help to delay the next pregnancy. However, there is some possibility – less than 2 per cent – that a mother can become pregnant before her periods return. This becomes increasingly likely after six months.

BREASTFEEDING

KEY MESSAGE

2.

Newborn babies should be given to the mother to hold immediately after delivery. They should have skin-to-skin contact with the mother and begin breastfeeding within one hour of birth.

SUPPORTING INFORMATION

Skin-to-skin contact and breastfeeding soon after birth stimulate production of the mother's breastmilk. Breastfeeding also helps the mother's womb contract, which reduces the risk of heavy bleeding or infection and helps to expel the placenta (afterbirth).

Colostrum, the thick yellowish milk the mother produces in the first few days after giving birth, is the perfect food for newborn babies. It is very nutritious and full of antibodies that help protect the baby against infections. Sometimes mothers are advised not to feed colostrum to their babies. *This advice is incorrect.* Newborns benefit from colostrum.

The newborn needs no other food or drink while the mother's milk supply is coming in and breastfeeding is being fully established. Giving any other food or drink may slow the production of milk. It can also increase the chance of diarrhoea and other infections. The milk produced by the mother is nutritious and the right amount for the newborn. The baby should breastfeed as often as she or he wants.

A baby who has problems suckling in the first few days should be kept close to the mother, offered the breast frequently, helped to take the breast and given breastmilk expressed directly into the mouth or fed expressed breastmilk from a clean cup (not from a bottle). The mother should receive help to improve the baby's attachment and suckling, and should also be shown how to express breastmilk, if necessary.

A mother's own milk is best for low-birthweight babies. However, not all of these infants are able to feed from the breast in the first days of life. For them, other options are available. In order of preference, they are: expressed breastmilk (from the mother); donor breastmilk (only if the donor is HIV-tested and the milk is correctly heat-treated); and infant formula. All of these should be given by cup, spoon or *paladai* (a cup feeding device), or medical tubes used by a trained health worker in a health facility.

Heat-treated breastmilk involves heating expressed breastmilk (enough for one or two feeds) in a small pan or in a metal container standing in a pan of water until it comes to a boil. The milk is then left to cool in a clean, covered container before it is fed to the baby by cup. A trained health worker can provide further guidance on expressing and heat-treating breastmilk.

It is best for the mother and her baby to stay together in the same room immediately after birth. If a mother gives birth in a hospital or clinic, she is entitled to have her baby near her, 24 hours a day. She should insist that no formula or water be given to her baby if she is breastfeeding.

3.

Almost every mother can breastfeed successfully. Breastfeeding the baby frequently causes production of more milk. The baby should breastfeed at least eight times daily, day and night, and on demand.

SUPPORTING INFORMATION

A mother's breasts make as much milk as the baby wants. If the baby suckles more, more milk is produced. Almost every mother can successfully breastfeed and produce enough milk when:

- she breastfeeds exclusively

- the baby is in a good position and is well attached to the breast, with the breast well in the baby's mouth

- the baby feeds as often and for as long as she or he wants, including during the night, and is kept on the breast until she or he has finished suckling. The baby should finish feeding from one breast before being fed from the other breast.

Holding the baby in a good position makes it easier for the baby to take the breast well into the mouth and suckle.

Signs that the baby is in a good position for breastfeeding are:

- the baby's head and body are in line
- the baby is close to the mother's body
- the baby's whole body is turned towards the mother
- the baby is relaxed, happy and suckling.

Holding the baby in a poor position can cause difficulties such as:

- sore and cracked nipples
- the baby does not receive enough milk
- the baby refuses to feed.

Signs that the baby is well attached:

- more of the dark skin around the mother's nipple (areola) can be seen above the baby's mouth than below it
- the baby's mouth is wide open
- the baby's lower lip is turned outward
- the baby's chin is touching the mother's breast.

Signs that the baby is suckling well:

- the baby takes long, deep sucks
- the cheeks are round when suckling
- the baby releases the breast when finished.

Generally, the mother does not feel any pain in her breast when breastfeeding.

From birth, the baby should breastfeed whenever she or he wants. A baby should be fed on demand at least eight times in a 24-hour period, during both the day and the night. If a newborn sleeps more than three hours after breastfeeding, she or he may be gently awakened and offered the breast.

Crying is not a sign that the baby needs other foods or drinks. It normally means the baby wants to be held and cuddled more, the baby's diaper or nappy needs changing, or the baby is too hot or cold. Some babies need to suckle the breast for comfort. More suckling produces more breastmilk, which helps satisfy the baby's feeding needs. If the baby cries a lot and does not settle after feeding and being cuddled, the mother may need additional breastfeeding support or the baby might not be well. A trained health worker should be consulted.

Using pacifiers, dummies or bottles can interfere with establishing breastfeeding in the baby's first months of life, as the sucking action for these is different from suckling at the breast. The baby may become used to the bottle teat or pacifier and refuse the breast. This may cause less suckling time at the breast, which reduces milk production. Pacifiers and bottle teats may become contaminated, increasing a baby's risk of illness.

Mothers who fear they do not have enough breastmilk often give their babies other food or drink in the first few months of life. This causes the baby to suckle less often, so less breastmilk is produced. The mother will produce more milk if she does not give the child other food or liquids and if she breastfeeds often.

Mothers need to be reassured that they can feed their babies under 6 months of age properly with breastmilk *alone*, and they need to be shown how to do it. All mothers, especially those lacking the confidence to breastfeed, need encouragement and support from the child's father and their families, neighbours, friends, health workers, employers and women's organizations. A mother who has undergone a Caesarean birth may require extra help to begin breastfeeding her baby.

Skilled birth attendants can raise awareness and understanding about the benefits of breastfeeding. They should support mothers to initiate and continue breastfeeding and help fathers and other family members accept breastfeeding as a natural and nutritious practice that protects the life of the baby.

4.

Breastfeeding helps protect babies and young children against dangerous illnesses. It also creates a special bond between mother and child.

SUPPORTING INFORMATION

Breastmilk is a baby's 'first immunization'. It helps to protect against diarrhoea, ear and chest infections, and other health problems. The protection is greatest when breastmilk *alone* is given for the first six months and when breastfeeding continues along with other foods well into the second year and beyond. No other milks, foods or supplements can provide the protection of breastmilk.

Breastfeeding helps a mother and baby form a close, loving relationship – a process called bonding. The close contact and attention help infants feel secure and loved, which is important for their growth and development.

The father and other family members can help by encouraging the mother to rest quietly while she breastfeeds the baby. They can also make sure the mother has enough nutritious food and help with household tasks and caring for older children.

5.

Bottle feeding and giving a baby breastmilk substitutes such as infant formula or animal milk can threaten the baby's health and survival. If a woman cannot breastfeed her infant, the baby can be fed expressed breastmilk or, if necessary, a quality breastmilk substitute from an ordinary clean cup.

SUPPORTING INFORMATION

Babies who do not receive breastmilk do not receive protection from illnesses provided by the mother's antibodies and other components that come in her milk. These babies are more likely to get diarrhoea and respiratory and ear infections. Diarrhoea and respiratory infections, such as pneumonia, can be deadly in babies and young children.

Feeding the baby breastmilk substitutes can cause poor growth or illness if (1) too much or too little water is added, (2) the water is not from a safe source and/or (3) the bottles and teats are not cleaned properly. Powdered breastmilk substitutes may contain harmful bacteria that can cause illness. Studies suggest that children fed breastmilk substitutes, as compared to breastfed children, are at greater risk of childhood obesity and some chronic illnesses, such as heart disease, later in life.

Feeding the baby breastmilk substitutes can be expensive and particularly risky if parents cannot afford to buy enough of a quality breastmilk substitute. For example, to feed one baby for the first six months requires 20 kilograms (about 40 tins) of infant formula. Trained health workers should inform all parents considering the use of breastmilk substitutes about the costs.

If it is necessary to feed the baby with formula, it is important to boil clean drinking water first and then add the hot water to the powdered formula. The water should not be added after it has cooled down. The directions for mixing should be carefully followed. This ensures that the right amounts of formula and safe water are mixed and that the process is hygienic. Before giving the formula to the baby, the mother, father or other caregiver must make sure it is not too hot.

Animal milk and infant formula go bad if left at room temperature (around 20–25 degrees Celsius) for more than two hours. Breastmilk can be stored for up to eight hours at room temperature without going bad. Of course, it is better to safely store all types of milk in a clean, covered container, preferably in a refrigerator.

Cup feeding is safer than bottle feeding because the cup can be easily cleaned with soap and water. Cup feeding also provides some of the contact and stimulation the baby needs, since the person has to hold the baby. Feeding with a cup does not cause problems with suckling at the breast.

The best food for a baby who cannot be breastfed directly is milk expressed from the mother's breast, given from a clean, open cup. Even newborn babies can be fed with an open cup. If it is necessary to feed a baby with a nutritionally adequate breastmilk substitute, it should be fed to the baby by cup.

KEY MESSAGE

6.

If a woman is infected with HIV, there is a risk that she can pass the infection to her infant through breastfeeding. In the first six months, this risk is much greater if the infant is fed both breastmilk and other liquids and foods than if fed breastmilk *alone*. Therefore, it is recommended that the baby receives breastmilk *alone* for the first six months, unless it is acceptable, feasible, affordable, sustainable and safe to give breastmilk substitutes (infant formula) exclusively.

SUPPORTING INFORMATION

HIV testing, treatment and counselling

Pregnant women and new mothers who think they may be infected with HIV should consult a trained health worker for HIV testing and counselling. Women who are HIV-positive should be counselled on how to reduce the risk of passing HIV to their children during pregnancy, childbirth or breastfeeding. They should also be counselled and supported on how to get treatment and care for themselves.

A trained health worker can provide women who are HIV-positive with information on antiretroviral therapy (ART), a group of medicines for people with HIV infection. ART can help reduce the risk of mother-to-child transmission of HIV and contribute to keeping the mother healthy.

All health workers should know if HIV testing and ART are available at their local clinic. They should provide information on these and other related services to pregnant women and new mothers.

The HIV-positive mother should be counselled and provided with information to help her decide which feeding option is best for her baby and most manageable for her. The HIV-positive mother should know that:

- if she breastfeeds exclusively during the first six months she reduces the baby's risk of illness, malnutrition and death
- if she uses breastmilk substitutes such as infant formula exclusively she avoids the risk of HIV infection through breastmilk
- shortening the duration of breastfeeding can reduce the risk of transmitting the infection to the infant.

The most appropriate infant feeding option for the child of an HIV-infected mother ultimately depends on individual circumstances. The mother needs to assess the risks through discussion with a trained health worker. The mother infected with HIV has the right to (1) the information she needs to make an informed decision and (2) all the services and support necessary to help her implement that decision.

Infant Feeding Options

The first six months:

- Feeding the baby with infant formula (breastmilk substitutes) should be considered only if it is acceptable, affordable, feasible, sustainable and safe for the mother and child. If all these conditions can be met, the baby can be fed a quality breastmilk substitute *alone* for the first six months, with no breastmilk or other foods. This eliminates the risk of passing HIV to the baby through breastfeeding.

- If the HIV-positive mother decides to breastfeed, she should feed her baby breastmilk *exclusively*, giving no other liquids, milks or foods, for the first six months. Feeding breastmilk *alone* in the first six months can reduce a baby's risk of HIV infection compared to giving both breastmilk and other foods and liquids ('mixed feeding').

- Mixed feeding not only greatly increases the risk of transmitting HIV to the baby in the first six months but also causes more illness, such as diarrhoea and pneumonia, and malnutrition, and increases the risk of death.

After six months:

- All infants should be started on other foods to meet their growing nutritional needs.

- Women who have breastfed their infants during the first six months should continue to give their babies breastmilk along with other foods unless they meet the conditions to give safe replacement foods, including

BREASTFEEDING

infant formula and other milks and foods. Once a nutritionally adequate and safe diet can be provided, all breastfeeding should stop.

Other Important Information

During counselling, a pregnant woman or new mother with HIV can be helped to determine whether she can provide her baby with a nutritionally adequate and safe diet without breastmilk. This assessment should be undertaken not only once, such as before the child is born, but also throughout the period of breastfeeding, with the support of the trained health worker.

If the mother is confident that she can provide sufficient amounts of a quality breastmilk substitute, properly and hygienically prepared with clean water, then she can opt to stop all breastfeeding and begin using the breastmilk substitute. A trained health worker should provide the mother and father with guidance on safe and clean practices to prepare the breastmilk substitute.

A new mother who does not know her HIV status should exclusively breastfeed her child for the first six months and continue breastfeeding for up to two years and beyond in addition to feeding the child other nutritious foods and drinks.

Infants confirmed as HIV-positive should be breastfed so they can receive the benefits of breastmilk.

(Refer to the HIV chapter for more information on children and families living with HIV.)

KEY MESSAGE

7.

A woman employed away from her home can continue to breastfeed her child. She should breastfeed as often as possible when she is with the infant and express her breastmilk when they are apart so that another caregiver can feed it to the baby in a clean and safe way.

SUPPORTING INFORMATION

If a mother cannot be with her baby during working hours, she should breastfeed often when they are together. With frequent breastfeeding, she will continue to produce breastmilk.

If a woman cannot breastfeed at her workplace, she can express her milk two or three times during the workday and refrigerate it or store it at room temperature for up to eight hours in a clean, covered container. The expressed milk can be given to the child by another caregiver from a clean cup.

Families and communities can encourage employers to provide paid maternity leave, crèches, and the time and a suitable place for women to breastfeed or express and store their milk. The place should be clean, safe and private. It should have clean water available for washing hands and utensils.

8.

After 6 months of age, when babies begin to eat foods, breastfeeding should continue for up to two years and beyond because it is an important source of nutrition, energy and protection from illness.

SUPPORTING INFORMATION

Breastmilk remains an important source of energy, protein and other nutrients such as vitamin A and iron, even when babies begin to consume additional foods after 6 months of age. Breastmilk helps protect a child against disease for as long as the child breastfeeds.

It is recommended that a mother continue to breastfeed her child up to two years and beyond – as long as she and the child wish to continue. Breastfeeding can comfort a child who is upset and is an important source of nourishment during a child's illness.

Why it is important to share and act on information about
NUTRITION AND GROWTH

More than one third of all child deaths every year around the world are attributed to malnutrition, specifically undernutrition, which weakens the body's resistance to illness.

If a woman is malnourished during pregnancy or if her child is malnourished during the first two years of life, the child's physical and mental growth and development will be slowed. This cannot be corrected when the child is older – it will affect the child for the rest of his or her life.

Malnutrition develops when the body does not get the proper amount of energy (calories), proteins, carbohydrates, fats, vitamins, minerals and other nutrients required to keep the organs and tissues healthy and functioning well. A child or adult can be malnourished by being undernourished or overnourished.

In most parts of the world malnutrition occurs when people are undernourished. Primary reasons for undernourishment, especially of children and women, are poverty, lack of food, repeated illnesses, inappropriate feeding practices, lack of care and poor hygiene. Undernourishment raises the risk of malnutrition. The risk is greatest in the first two years of life. The risk further increases when diarrhoea and other illnesses sap the body of the proteins, minerals and nutrients required to stay healthy.

When a household does not have enough food and has conditions that make diarrhoea and other illnesses common, children are the most vulnerable to becoming malnourished. When children become sick, they lose energy and nutrients quickly, which puts their lives at risk faster than adults.

Overnutrition is when a person is overweight or obese. It can cause diabetes in childhood and cardiovascular disease and other diseases in adulthood. Sometimes children eat large quantities of foods that are high in energy but not rich in other necessary nutrients, such as sugary drinks or fried, starchy foods. In such cases improving the quality of the child's diet is crucial along with increasing his or her level of physical activity.

Children with chronic diseases, such as HIV, are even more susceptible to malnutrition. Their bodies have a harder time absorbing vitamins, iron and other nutrients. Children with disabilities may need extra attention to make sure they get the nutrition they need.

All girls and boys have the right to a caring and protective environment, with mothers, fathers or other caregivers making sure they are well nourished with a healthy diet.

NUTRITION AND GROWTH

KEY MESSAGES:
What every family and community
has a right to know about

NUTRITION AND GROWTH

1. A young child should grow and gain weight rapidly. From birth to age 2, children should be weighed regularly to assess growth. If regular weighing shows that the child is not gaining weight, or the parents or other caregivers see the child is not growing, something is wrong. The child needs to be seen by a trained health worker.

2. Breastmilk *alone* is the only food and drink an infant needs in the first six months of life. After six months, a baby needs a *variety* of other foods in addition to breastmilk to ensure healthy growth and development.

3. From the age of 6–8 months a child needs to eat two to three times per day and three to four times per day starting at 9 months – in addition to breastfeeding. Depending on the child's appetite, one or two nutritious snacks, such as fruit or bread with nut paste, may be needed between meals. The baby should be fed small amounts of food that steadily increase in *variety* and *quantity* as he or she grows.

4. Feeding times are periods of learning, love and interaction, which promote physical, social and emotional growth and development. The parent or other caregiver should talk to children during feeding, and treat and feed girls and boys equally and patiently.

5. Children need vitamin A to help resist illness, protect their eyesight and reduce the risk of death. Vitamin A can be found in many fruits and vegetables, red palm oil, eggs, dairy products, liver, fish, meat, fortified foods and breastmilk. In areas where vitamin A deficiency is common, high-dose vitamin A supplements can also be given every four to six months to children aged 6 months to 5 years.

6. Children need iron-rich foods to protect their physical and mental abilities and to prevent anaemia. The best sources of iron are animal sources, such as liver, lean meats and fish. Other good sources are iron-fortified foods and iron supplements.

7. Iodine in a pregnant woman's and young child's diet is especially critical for the development of the child's brain. It is essential to help prevent learning disabilities and delayed development. Using iodized salt instead of ordinary salt provides pregnant women and their children with as much iodine as they need.

8. As the child's intake of foods and drinks increases, the risk of diarrhoea substantially increases. Contamination of foods with germs is a major cause of diarrhoea and other illnesses that cause children to lose nutrients and energy needed for growth and development. Good hygiene, safe water and proper handling, preparation and storing of foods are crucial to prevent illnesses.

9. During an illness, children need additional fluids and encouragement to eat regular meals, and breastfeeding infants need to breastfeed more often. After an illness, children need to be offered more food than usual to replenish the energy and nourishment lost due to the illness.

10. Very thin and/or swollen children need special medical care. They should be taken to a trained health worker or health facility for assessment and treatment.

NUTRITION AND GROWTH

Supporting Information

KEY MESSAGE

1. A young child should grow and gain weight rapidly. From birth to age 2, children should be weighed regularly to assess growth. If regular weighing shows that the child is not gaining weight, or the parents or other caregivers see the child is not growing, something is wrong. The child needs to be seen by a trained health worker.

SUPPORTING INFORMATION

Weight gain is the most important sign that a child is healthy and is growing and developing well. From birth to 1 year of age, infants should be weighed at least once every month. From 1–2 years of age they should be weighed at least once every three months.

Whenever a child visits a health centre, he or she should be weighed. This can help early detection of faltering growth so appropriate actions can be taken.

A health check-up can also detect if a child is gaining weight too fast for his or her age. This requires examining a child's weight in relation to his or her height, which can determine if the child is overweight.

If the child is underweight or overweight, it is important to examine the child's diet and provide the parents or other caregiver with advice on good nutrition. Increasingly there are undernourished and overnourished people side by side in a family.

A child who is given only breastmilk for the first six months usually grows well during this time. Breastfeeding helps protect babies from common illnesses and ensures good physical and mental growth and development. Infants who are breastfed tend to learn more readily than infants who are fed other kinds of milk.

From the age of 6 months, a child needs to start eating a variety of other nutritious foods, in addition to breastmilk, to ensure healthy growth and development.

Every child should have a growth chart that tracks his or her growth. It shows whether the child is growing appropriately for his or her age. At each weighing the child's weight should be marked with a dot on the growth chart and the dots should be connected. This will produce a line that shows how well the child is growing. If the line goes up, the child is doing well. A line that stays flat or goes down is a cause for concern.

Children need to gain not only adequate weight but also adequate height. A child's height can also be tracked on a chart. Good nutrition, care and hygiene, especially in the first two years of life, are necessary to prevent children from becoming too short for their age (stunted). If a mother is undernourished or does not have proper nutrition during pregnancy, her child may be born too small. This puts the child at risk of becoming stunted later on. A low-birthweight baby needs additional attention to feeding and care to grow adequately.

A child who is not gaining enough weight over one or two months may need larger servings, more nutritious food or more frequent meals. The child may be sick or may need more attention and care or assistance with eating. Parents and trained health workers need to act quickly to discover the cause of the problem and take steps to correct it.

Here are some important questions to ask to help identify growth problems:

- **Is the child eating often enough?** In addition to breastfeeding, a child aged 6–8 months needs to eat two to three times per day and three to four times per day starting at 9 months. Additional nutritious snacks, such as a piece of fruit or bread with nut paste, may be needed one or two times per day. A child with developmental delays or disabilities may require extra help and time for feeding.

- **Is the child receiving enough food?** A child aged 6–8 months needs to receive initially 2–3 spoonfuls of food, increasing gradually to ½ cup (250-millilitre), at each meal. A child 9–12 months old needs to receive ½ cup at each meal. A child 12–23 months old requires ¾ to 1 whole cup of 'family foods' at each meal. Children 2 years and older need to receive at least 1 whole cup at each meal. If the child finishes his or her food and wants more, the child needs to be offered more.

- **Do the child's meals have too little 'growth' or 'energy' foods?** Foods that help children grow are beans, nuts, meat, fish, eggs, dairy products, grains and pulses. The daily inclusion of animal-source foods in the diet is particularly important. A small amount of oil can add energy. Red palm oil or other vitamin-enriched edible oils are good sources of energy.

High-quality 'growth' foods are especially important to ensure that children gain both adequate weight and height. Foods such as highly processed fatty foods or sugary snacks are not rich in vitamins and minerals and other important nutrients and may cause children to gain too much weight without a proportionate growth in height.

- **Is the child refusing to eat?** If the child does not seem to like the taste of a particular food, other foods should be offered. New foods should be introduced gradually.

- **Is the child sick?** A sick child needs encouragement to eat small, frequent meals. The child needs to be breastfed more frequently. After an illness, the child needs to eat more than usual to regain the weight lost and to replenish energy and nourishment. If the child is frequently ill, he or she should be checked by a trained health worker.

- **Is the child getting enough foods with vitamin A?** Breastmilk is rich in vitamin A. Other foods with vitamin A are liver, eggs, dairy products, red palm oil, yellow and orange fruits and vegetables, and green leafy vegetables. If these foods are not available in adequate amounts, a health-care provider can provide the child with a vitamin A supplement (tablet or syrup) every four to six months.

- **Is the child being given breastmilk substitutes by bottle?** If a breastmilk substitute is given, it should be fed from a clean, open cup, rather than from a bottle.

- **Is the food kept clean?** If not, the child will often be ill. Raw food should be washed or cooked with clean water from a safe source. Cooked food should be eaten without delay. Leftover food should be carefully stored and thoroughly reheated.

- **Is the water kept clean?** Clean water is vital for a child's health. Water should come from a safe source and be kept clean by storing it in covered containers that are clean on the inside and outside. Clean drinking water can be obtained from a regularly maintained, controlled and chlorinated piped supply, public standpipe, borehole, protected dug well, protected spring or rainwater collection. If water is drawn from ponds, streams, unprotected springs, wells or tanks, it needs to be purified. Home water treatments can be used such as boiling, filtering, adding chlorine or disinfecting with sunlight in accordance with information provided by a trained health worker or extension agent.

- **Are faeces being put in a latrine or toilet or buried? Are hands being washed with soap and water or a substitute, such as ash and water, after use of the latrine or toilet?** If not, the child may frequently get worms and other sicknesses. A child with worms needs deworming medicine from a trained health worker.

- **Is the young child left alone much of the time or in the care of an older child?** If so, the young child may need more attention and interaction from adults, especially during mealtime.

2.

Breastmilk *alone* is the only food and drink an infant needs in the first six months of life. After six months, a baby needs a *variety* of other foods in addition to breastmilk to ensure healthy growth and development.

SUPPORTING INFORMATION

In the first six months, when a baby is most at risk, exclusive breastfeeding helps to protect against diarrhoea and other common infections and gets the baby off to a good start in life.

At 6 months of age, the child needs other foods and drinks in addition to breastmilk. These provide energy, protein, vitamins and other nutrients needed to support growth and development.

A variety of foods – vegetables and fruits, meat, poultry, fish, eggs and dairy products – help to meet the child's nutrition needs. Breastfeeding for up to two years and beyond provides an important source of nutrients that protect against disease.

If soft, semi-solid or solid foods are introduced too late, the child may not be getting the necessary nutrients. This can slow down growth and development.

When introducing solid foods, it is important to start with soft, mushy foods and move gradually to more solid foods. The greater the variety of healthy foods, the more balanced and nutritious the child's diet.

The consistency and variety of foods should be adapted to a child's requirements and eating abilities. At 6 months of age infants can eat pureed or mashed foods, thick soups and porridges. By 8 months most infants can also eat 'finger foods' (snacks that children can eat by themselves). By 12 months, most children can eat the same types of foods as the rest of the family.

Parents or other caregivers should avoid giving foods that may cause choking, such as nuts, grapes and raw carrots and other foods that have a shape and/or consistency that may cause them to become lodged in the child's throat.

It may be difficult to meet all the child's nutrient requirements without a lot of foods from animal sources. So it may be necessary to give the child fortified foods or spreads or multiple vitamin and mineral supplements, such as powders, syrups or dissolvable tablets. A trained health worker can advise the parent or other caregiver about foods that provide the most nutrients and which supplements to use.

NUTRITION AND GROWTH

Following are some nutritious foods for young children (older than six months) to eat:

- Staple foods, including cereals (rice, wheat, maize, millet, quinoa), roots (cassava, yam, potatoes) and starchy fruits (plantain and breadfruit).

- High-protein foods, such as red meat, poultry, fish, liver and eggs (can be given as often as possible).

- Dairy products, such as cheese, yogurt, curds and dried milk (which can be mixed with other foods, such as cooked porridge). These are good choices in the second six months of a breastfed child's life. These are better choices than raw milk, which is harder for the child to digest.

- Green leafy and orange-coloured vegetables, such as spinach, broccoli, chard, carrots, pumpkins and sweet potatoes (which provide vitamins).

- Pulses, such as chickpeas, lentils, cowpeas, black-eyed peas, kidney beans and lima beans (to add variety and provide protein, energy and some iron).

- Oils, especially rapeseed oil, soy oil, red palm oil, butter or margarine.

- Seeds, including groundnut paste, other nut pastes and soaked or germinated seeds, such as pumpkin, sunflower, melon or sesame seeds (for energy and some vitamins).

It is difficult to provide all the nutrients needed by young children in a vegetarian diet. This is because foods from animal sources provide key nutrients, such as iron. A child eating a vegetarian diet needs additional nutrients in the form of multiple vitamin tablets or powders, fortified spreads or nutrient-rich food supplements.

Iron from plant foods is generally not absorbed very well by the body. However, plant foods such as pulses (white beans, chickpeas, lentils) have more iron. The iron will be better absorbed if eaten together with foods that are high in vitamin C, such as oranges and other citrus fruits and juices.

KEY MESSAGE

3.

From the age of 6–8 months a child needs to eat two to three times per day and three to four times per day starting at 9 months, in addition to breastfeeding. Depending on the child's appetite, one or two nutritious snacks, such as fruit or bread with nut paste, may be needed between meals. The baby should be fed small amounts of food that steadily increase in *variety* and *quantity* as he or she grows.

SUPPORTING INFORMATION

Good nutrition in the first two years of life is crucial. Inadequate nutrition during this period can slow a child's physical and mental development for the rest of his or her life.

In order to grow and stay healthy, young children need a variety of nutritious foods such as meat, fish, pulses, grains, eggs, fruits and vegetables, as well as breastmilk.

A child's stomach is smaller than an adult's, so a child cannot eat as much at one meal. However, children's energy and body-building needs are great. It is important that children eat frequently to provide for all their needs.

Foods such as mashed vegetables and chopped meat, eggs or fish should be added to the child's diet as often as possible. A small amount of oil may be added, preferably vitamin-enriched oil.

If meals are served in a common dish, younger children may not get enough food. Giving a young child his or her own plate or bowl makes it easier for the parent or other caregiver to know what foods and how much the child has eaten.

Young children may need to be encouraged to eat, and they may need help in handling food or utensils. A child with a developmental delay or disability may need extra help eating and drinking.

The following gives information on how often and how much a young child should be fed:

6–8 months:

Children should breastfeed frequently and receive other foods two to three times a day. Parents should start with soft or mushy foods (such as porridge) and gradually increase the consistency (thickness) of food. Animal foods such as meat, eggs and fish can be given as early as possible, but they should be mashed, minced or cut into very small pieces. Start with 2–3 spoonfuls per feeding, increasing gradually to ½ of a 250-millilitre cup.

9–24 months:

Children should receive other foods three to four times a day in addition to breastfeeding. Give infants aged 9–11 months ½ of a 250-millilitre cup per feeding. Provide children aged 12–23 months ¾ to 1 whole 250-millilitre cup per feeding. Give children 2 years and older at least 1 whole 250-millilitre cup per feeding. Foods from animals, such as meat, fish and eggs, should be included as much as possible.

By 12 months:

Most children are able to consume 'family foods' of a solid consistency. They can still be offered semi-solid foods, which are easier for young children to eat. Additional nutritious snacks (such as fruit, bread or bread with nut paste) can be offered once or twice per day, as desired, starting at six months. If the quality or amount of food per meal is low, or the child is no longer breastfeeding, give 1–2 cups of milk plus one or two extra meals each day.

4.

Feeding times are periods of learning, love and interaction, which promote physical, social and emotional growth and development. The parent or other caregiver should talk to children during feeding, and treat and feed girls and boys equally and patiently.

SUPPORTING INFORMATION

Mealtimes provide the opportunity for mothers and fathers or other caregivers to interact and talk with children and support their learning. This helps to stimulate social and emotional development.

It is important to encourage children to eat, but not to force-feed them. Each child's needs vary due to differences in breastmilk intake and variability in growth rate. Infants need to be fed directly. Young children should be assisted when they are learning to feed themselves.

If a child refuses to eat a variety of foods, the caregiver can experiment with different food combinations, tastes, textures and methods of encouragement. The caregiver should minimize distractions during meals if the child loses interest easily.

Girls and boys require the same amount of attention and time for feeding. They should receive the same quantity and quality of food and drink. They both need to be breastfed for the first six months and receive an adequate variety and quantity of foods after six months. It is important for both mothers and fathers to be informed about child nutrition. Both parents should take part in feeding their daughters and sons.

KEY MESSAGE

5.

Children need vitamin A to help resist illness, protect their eyesight and reduce the risk of death. Vitamin A can be found in many fruits and vegetables, red palm oil, eggs, dairy products, liver, fish, meat, fortified foods and breastmilk. In areas where vitamin A deficiency is common, high-dose vitamin A supplements can also be given every four to six months to children aged 6 months to 5 years.

SUPPORTING INFORMATION

Until infants are 6 months old, breastmilk is the main source of vitamin A, provided the mother has enough vitamin A from her diet or supplements. Children aged 6 months to 5 years can get vitamin A from a variety of other foods, such as liver, eggs, dairy products, fatty fish, red palm oil, ripe mangoes and papayas, oranges, yellow sweet potatoes, dark green leafy vegetables and carrots.

When children do not have enough vitamin A they are less able to fight potentially fatal diseases and are at risk of night blindness. A child who has difficulty seeing in the early evening and at night is probably deficient in vitamin A. The child should be taken to a trained health worker for treatment with high-dose vitamin A supplements.

In a few countries, vitamin A has been added to cooking oils, sugar, wheat and flours, milk and dairy products, and other foods. In many countries where vitamin A deficiency is widespread and children often die from illnesses such as diarrhoea and measles, vitamin A is distributed twice a year to children 6 months to 5 years of age in a high-dose capsule or syrup.

Diarrhoea and measles deplete vitamin A from the child's body. A child with diarrhoea lasting several days or with measles, or who is severely malnourished, should be treated with high-dose vitamin A supplements obtained from a trained health worker.

In areas where it is known or suspected that children suffer from vitamin A deficiency, those children with diarrhoea should be given a vitamin A supplement if they have not received one within the past month, or if they are not already receiving vitamin A at regular four to six month intervals.

Children with measles should receive vitamin A on the day of diagnosis, a dose on the following day and another dose at least two weeks later.

Zinc (tablet or syrup) can also be given for 10–14 days to reduce the severity and the duration of the diarrhoea as well as protect the child for up to two months from future diarrhoea episodes. The dosage for children over 6 months of age is 20 milligrams per day, for children under 6 months of age it is 10 milligrams per day.

KEY MESSAGE

6.

Children need iron-rich foods to protect their physical and mental abilities and to prevent anaemia. The best sources of iron are animal sources, such as liver, lean meats and fish. Other good sources are iron-fortified foods and iron supplements.

SUPPORTING INFORMATION

A lack of iron in the diet is a common cause of anaemia. Children can also become anaemic from malaria and hookworm. Iron deficiency can impair physical and mental development in infants and young children. Even mild iron deficiency can impair intellectual development. Anaemia is the most common nutritional disorder in the world.

Iron is found in animal foods such as liver, lean meats and fish. It is also in some vegetarian foods such as pulses. Foods such as wheat and maize flours, salt, fish sauce or soy sauce are sometimes fortified with iron. Iron-rich foods help prevent anaemia. Consuming them with vitamin C helps the digestive system to better absorb the iron.

NUTRITION AND GROWTH

Symptoms of anaemia include paleness of the palms of the hands and of the tongue and inside the eyelids and lips as well as tiredness and breathlessness.

- In children under 2 years of age:

    Anaemia may cause problems with coordination and balance, and the child may appear withdrawn and hesitant. This can limit the child's ability to interact and may hinder intellectual development.

    The child can benefit from iron-containing vitamin and mineral preparations, such as supplements and multiple vitamin and mineral powders. These powders can be easily mixed by the caregiver in home-prepared foods for children older than 6 months.

- In pregnant women and adolescent girls:

    Anaemia increases the severity of haemorrhage and the risk of infection during childbirth. It is an important cause of maternal mortality. Infants born to anaemic mothers often suffer from low birthweight and anaemia.

    Iron supplements for pregnant women protect both the mothers and their babies. Adolescent girls who are anaemic will also benefit from a weekly iron-folic acid supplement to build their iron stores and prepare their bodies for healthy pregnancies.

Malaria and hookworm can be main causes of anaemia. Taking iron supplements to treat anaemia while having malaria can worsen the anaemia.

With regard to malaria:

- Children living in malarial areas should not take iron and folic acid preparations, including iron-containing powders, unless the malaria has been diagnosed and treated and they have been screened for anaemia.

- In general, children living in malarial areas should not be given preventive doses of iron-containing vitamin and mineral preparations or supplements unless they are delivered through a fortified food.

- Pregnant women, mothers, fathers and other caregivers living in malarial areas need to ask a trained health worker about using iron supplements for their children.

- To help prevent malaria, children, pregnant women, and mothers and other family members should sleep under insecticide-treated mosquito nets.

With regard to worms:

- Children living in areas where worms are highly endemic should be treated two to three times a year with a recommended deworming (anthelmintic) medication. Deworming the child regularly helps treat the anaemia caused by worms and also helps children regain their appetite. Good hygiene practices prevent worms. Children should not play near the latrine, should wash their hands often with soap and water or a substitute, such as ash and water, and should wear shoes or sandals to prevent worm infestations.

- Pregnant women living in areas where worms are common should be treated with a recommended deworming medication.

7.

Iodine in a pregnant woman's and young child's diet is especially critical for the development of the child's brain. It is essential to help prevent learning disabilities and delayed development. Using iodized salt instead of ordinary salt provides pregnant women and their children with as much iodine as they need.

SUPPORTING INFORMATION

Small amounts of iodine are essential for children's growth and development. If a woman does not have enough iodine during pregnancy, her child is likely to be born with a mental disability or possibly a hearing or speech disability. If the child does not get enough iodine during infancy and childhood, he or she may have delayed physical, mental or cognitive development. Even mild deficiency can reduce learning ability and lower intelligence.

Goitre, an abnormal enlargement of the thyroid gland causing a swelling of the neck, is a sign of iodine missing in the diet. Iodine deficiency in early pregnancy increases the risk of miscarriage or stillbirth.

Using iodized salt instead of ordinary salt provides pregnant women and children with as much iodine as they need. Iodized salt is safe for the whole family and is the only salt needed for all cooking. Families should be sure to buy only iodized salt of good quality – properly marked and packaged. Mothers need to make sure they consume only iodized salt before, during and after pregnancy. Mothers and fathers need to ensure that the salt consumed by their children is iodized.

8.

As the child's intake of foods and drinks increases, the risk of diarrhoea substantially increases. Contamination of foods with germs is a major cause of diarrhoea and other illnesses that cause children to lose nutrients and energy needed for growth and development. Good hygiene, safe water and proper handling, preparation and storing of foods are crucial to prevent illnesses.

SUPPORTING INFORMATION

As children grow and become mobile they put everything in their mouths. They can pick up germs more easily as they explore and discover the world around them. This makes it very important for parents and other caregivers to practice good hygiene, such as hand washing with soap. They also need to handle and prepare food properly, use safe water and keep the living environment clean. These practices are important to prevent diarrhoea and other illnesses and to protect a child's health.

Foods should be served immediately after preparation and leftovers safely stored. Clean utensils and surfaces should be used to prepare and serve food. Children should be fed with clean cups and bowls. Bottles and nipples/teats should be avoided because they are difficult to keep clean.

Five key ways to keep food safe are: keep it clean; separate raw and cooked foods; cook food thoroughly; keep it at a safe temperature; and wash raw food materials in safe water.

(*Refer to the Hygiene chapter for more information.*)

KEY MESSAGE

9.

During an illness, children need additional fluids and encouragement to eat regular meals, and breastfeeding infants need to breastfeed more often. After an illness, children need to be offered more food than usual to replenish the energy and nourishment lost due to the illness.

SUPPORTING INFORMATION

When children are sick, such as when they have diarrhoea, measles or pneumonia, their appetite decreases and their body uses food less effectively. If the child is sick several times a year, his or her growth will slow or stop.

It is very important to encourage a sick child to eat. This can be difficult, as children who are ill may not be hungry. The parent or other caregiver should keep offering foods the child likes, a little at a time and as often as possible. Extra breastfeeding is especially important since it can provide nutrients required for recovery from infections.

It is essential to encourage a sick child to drink as often as possible. Dehydration (lack of fluids in the body) is a serious problem for children with diarrhoea. Drinking plenty of liquids will help prevent dehydration. When a child has diarrhoea, giving him or her oral rehydration salts (ORS) dissolved in clean water, along with foods and liquids, can help prevent dehydration. Giving the child a zinc supplement every day for 10–14 days can reduce the severity of the diarrhoea. The child is not fully recovered from an illness until he or she weighs about as much as when the illness began.

A child can die from persistent diarrhoea if it is not treated quickly. If diarrhoea and poor appetite persist for more than a few days, the mother, father or other caregiver needs to consult a trained health worker.

(*Refer to the Diarrhoea chapter for more information.*)

10.

Very thin and/or swollen children need special medical care. They should be taken to a trained health worker or health facility for assessment and treatment.

A short period of inadequate nutrition together with illness or infection can quickly make a child dangerously malnourished. The child needs urgent treatment with special foods and medicine. He or she should be taken directly to the nearest health-care provider.

Children with severe acute malnutrition are very thin. They may also have swollen parts of the body, usually the feet and the legs. A trained health worker can identify severe acute malnutrition by measuring the child's weight and height, using a special band to measure the upper arms or checking for equal swelling in both legs.

Treating a child with severe acute malnutrition effectively needs to be done by a health-care provider. The treatment depends on how sick the child is. Most children over 6 months old can be treated with a special ready-to-use therapeutic food (RUTF). This is a soft pre-packaged food that contains all the nutrients needed for the child's recovery. RUTF is easy for children to consume directly from the packet and requires no mixing with water or other foods, making it safe to use anywhere. Parents or other caregivers are provided with a week's supply of RUTF, along with information on how to treat the child. Medications are also provided as part of the treatment. The child should be taken back to the health-care provider every week to monitor his or her progress.

More intensive treatment is needed for children who are not able to eat RUTF, have other medical problems or are under 6 months old. These cases should be referred to a hospital or other facility that can provide 24-hour medical care, therapeutic milks and breastfeeding support.

Children with severe acute malnutrition get cold more quickly than other children, so they must always be kept warm. Skin-to-skin contact with the mother or other caregiver can help keep a child warm. Both the mother and child should be covered. The child's head should also be kept covered.

Although children with severe acute malnutrition need special nutritional treatment, breastmilk is still a vital source of nutrients and protection from disease. In addition to the special treatment (either at home or in a facility), children who are breastfeeding should continue to breastfeed.

Why it is important to share and act on information about
IMMUNIZATION

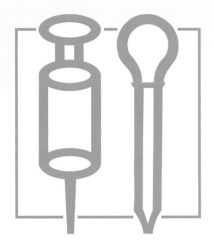

Each year, over 1.4 million children die from diseases that are preventable with readily available vaccines.[2]

These diseases include measles, meningitis caused by *Haemophilus influenzae* type B (Hib), diphtheria, tetanus, pertussis (whooping cough), yellow fever, polio and hepatitis B. New vaccines against other illnesses, such as pneumonia and diarrhoea caused by rotavirus, have been developed and are now more widely used.

Children who are immunized are protected from these dangerous diseases, which can often lead to disability or death. All children have the right to this protection.

Every girl and boy needs to be fully immunized. Early protection is critical. The immunizations in the child's first year and into the second year are especially important. It is also essential that pregnant women are immunized against tetanus to protect themselves as well as their newborns.

Although there has been progress in the past years in immunizing children, in 2008 nearly 24 million children — almost 20% of children born each year — did not get the routine immunizations scheduled for the first year of life.

Parents or other caregivers need to know why immunization is important, the recommended immunization schedule, and where their children can be immunized.

Parents or other caregivers need to know that it is safe to immunize a child who has a minor illness or a disability or is suffering from malnutrition.

2   As of 2002 (latest data available).

1. Immunization is urgent. Every child should complete the recommended series of immunizations. Early protection is critical; the immunizations in the first year and into the second year are especially important. All parents or other caregivers should follow the advice of a trained health worker on when to complete the required immunizations.

2. Immunization protects against several dangerous diseases. A child who is not immunized is more likely to become sick, permanently disabled or undernourished, and could possibly die.

3. It is safe to immunize a child who has a minor illness or a disability or is malnourished.

4. All pregnant women and their newborns need to be protected against tetanus. Even if a woman was immunized earlier, she needs to check with a trained health worker for advice on tetanus toxoid immunization.

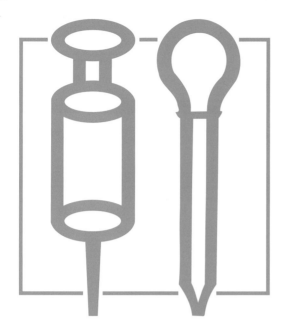

5. A new syringe must be used for every person being immunized. People should demand a new syringe for every vaccination.

6. Disease can spread quickly when people are crowded together. All children living in congested conditions, particularly in refugee or disaster situations, should be immunized immediately, especially against measles.

7. The vaccination card of a child (or an adult) should be presented to the health worker before every immunization.

IMMUNIZATION

KEY MESSAGE

1. Immunization is urgent. Every child should complete the recommended series of immunizations. Early protection is critical; the immunizations in the first year and into the second year are especially important. All parents or other caregivers should follow the advice of a trained health worker on when to complete the required immunizations.

SUPPORTING INFORMATION

Children must be immunized early in life. It is essential that infants, both girls and boys, get all recommended vaccines at the right time. Some vaccines require multiple doses for full protection. It is important for every child to complete the *full* number of these immunizations.

To protect the child during and beyond the first year of life, the immunizations in the following chart are necessary. These are most effective when given at the ages specified, or as close to those ages as possible.

Immunization schedule for infants[3]

Age at immunization	Location	Immunization
At birth	All countries	BCG[4]
	Some countries	Hepatitis B, polio
6–8 weeks	All countries	DTP[5] (also known as DPT), polio
	Most countries	Hepatitis B and Hib
	Some countries	Pneumococcal (conjugate), rotavirus
10–12 weeks	All countries	DTP, polio
	Most countries	Hepatitis B and Hib
	Some countries	Pneumococcal (conjugate), rotavirus
14–24 weeks	All countries	DTP, polio
	Most countries	Hepatitis B and Hib
	Some countries	Pneumococcal (conjugate), rotavirus[6]
9 months	Some countries	Yellow fever
9–15 months	All countries	Measles
12–18 months	Some countries	Mumps and rubella
15 months– 6 years	All countries	Measles[7]

3   Parents, caregivers and health workers should follow the national immunization schedule.
4   BCG (Bacille Calmette-Guérin) vaccine offers partial protection against some forms of tuberculosis and leprosy.
5   DTP (DPT) protects against diphtheria, tetanus and pertussis (whooping cough); many countries use DTPHepBHib, a five-in-one combination, vaccine also known as a pentavalent vaccine.
6   This is only for those receiving Rotateq™ vaccine, which has a three-dose schedule. A two-dose schedule is recommended for the Rotarix™ vaccine.
7   A minimum gap of one month should be given between the first and second doses of measles vaccine.

As new vaccines become available, more vaccines are recommended for all countries. But some vaccines are only needed in countries where certain diseases are present.

Parents and health workers should follow the locally recommended immunization schedule.

If a child does not complete the full series of immunizations in the first and into the second year of life, it is extremely important to have the child fully immunized as soon as possible. This can be done during special campaigns.

In some countries, additional vaccine doses, called 'booster shots', are offered after the first year of life. These help to sustain the effectiveness of the vaccine so the child is protected longer.

2.

Immunization protects against several dangerous diseases. A child who is not immunized is more likely to become sick, permanently disabled or undernourished, and could possibly die.

SUPPORTING INFORMATION

Immunization protects children against some of the most dangerous diseases of childhood. All children, including those who are disabled, need to be vaccinated. A child is immunized by vaccines, which are injected or given by mouth. The vaccines work by building up the child's defences against diseases. Immunization only works if given *before* the disease strikes.

A child who is not immunized is very likely to get measles, whooping cough and many other diseases that can kill. Children who survive these diseases are weakened and may not grow well. They may be permanently disabled. They may die later from malnutrition and other illnesses.

All children need to be immunized with BCG (Bacille Calmette-Guérin) vaccine, which offers partial protection against some forms of tuberculosis and leprosy.

All children need to be immunized against diphtheria, tetanus and pertussis with DTP vaccine (also known as DPT vaccine). Diphtheria causes infection of the upper respiratory tract, which in severe cases may lead to breathing difficulties and death. Tetanus causes rigid muscles and painful muscle spasms and can be deadly. Pertussis, or whooping cough, affects the respiratory tract and can cause a cough that lasts four to eight weeks. The disease is very dangerous in infants.

All pregnant women and infants need to be immunized against tetanus.

- Immunizing a woman or adolescent with at least two doses of tetanus toxoid before or during pregnancy protects the newborn for the first few weeks of life and protects the mother.

- At 6 weeks old, a baby needs the first dose of tetanus toxoid (the tetanus component of the DTP (DPT) vaccine) to extend the protection received from the mother against tetanus.

All children need to be immunized against measles, which can be a major cause of malnutrition, poor mental development, and hearing and visual impairments. The signs that a child has measles are a fever and rash, together with a cough, a runny nose or red eyes. A child can die from measles.

All children need to be immunized against polio. The signs of polio are a floppy limb or the inability to move. For every 200 children infected, one will be disabled for life.

In countries where hepatitis B is a problem, up to 10 out of every 100 children will harbour the infection for life if they are not immunized with hepatitis B vaccine. Up to one quarter of children infected with hepatitis B may develop serious liver conditions such as cancer when they are older.

In many countries, pneumonia caused by pneumococcus bacteria or *Haemophilus influenzae* type B (Hib) bacteria is common and kills many young children. Either of these bacteria can also cause childhood meningitis and other serious infections. These bacteria are among the most dangerous for children, particularly those under 5 years old. Vaccination with *Haemophilus influenzae* type B vaccine (Hib vaccine) and pneumococcal (conjugate) vaccine (PCV) can prevent these deaths.

A pentavalent vaccine (five vaccines in one), combining the DTP (DPT), hepatitis B and Hib vaccines, is increasingly being used by national immunization programmes.

Diarrhoea caused by rotavirus is common and can be severe. It affects nearly every child under age 5. Severe rotavirus diarrhoea is more common in developing countries where health care can be more difficult to access, resulting in many deaths in children under 5 years old, especially children under 2. Vaccination against rotavirus prevents diarrhoea caused by this virus. However, diarrhoea due to other bacteria or viruses can still occur in children who receive the rotavirus vaccine.

In some countries, yellow fever puts the lives of many young children and adults at risk. Vaccination can prevent the disease.

Japanese encephalitis virus is spread by mosquitoes, mainly in rural areas of Asian countries. It causes a severe illness, killing up to one third of those affected. Many survivors have brain damage. A trained health worker should be consulted for advice and information on national guidelines regarding use of this vaccine.

Breastmilk and colostrum, the thick yellow milk produced during the first few days after a woman gives birth, provide protection against diarrhoea, pneumonia and other diseases. Colostrum is sometimes referred to as a newborn's 'first vaccine', helping to build the child's immunity to disease.

In many countries where vitamin A deficiency is common, high-dose vitamin A capsules (or syrup) are administered to each child aged 6 months to 5 years, every four to six months. Vitamin A is distributed during routine immunization (such as with measles vaccine at 9 months) as well as during special immunization campaigns. Vitamin A is also an important part of measles treatment.

KEY MESSAGE

3.

It is safe to immunize a child who has a minor illness or a disability or is malnourished.

SUPPORTING INFORMATION

Many parents do not take a child to be immunized because the child has a fever, cough, cold, diarrhoea or some other illness. However, it is safe to immunize a child who has a minor illness.

It is also safe to immunize a child who has a disability or is malnourished. If a child is HIV-positive or suspected to be HIV-positive, a trained health worker should be consulted about which vaccines to give the child.

After an injection, the child may cry or develop a fever, a minor rash or a small sore. This is normal and shows that the vaccine is working. Children under 6 months of age should breastfeed frequently; older children should be given plenty of liquids and foods. If the child develops a high fever (over 38 degrees Celsius) the child should be taken to a trained health worker or health centre.

Measles can be extremely dangerous for malnourished children, so they should be immunized against measles, especially if the malnutrition is severe.

KEY MESSAGE

4.

All pregnant women and their newborns need to be protected against tetanus. Even if a woman was immunized earlier, she needs to check with a trained health worker for advice on tetanus toxoid immunization.

SUPPORTING INFORMATION

In many parts of the world, mothers give birth in unhygienic conditions. This puts both the mother and the child at risk of getting tetanus, a major killer of newborn infants.

If a pregnant woman is not immunized against tetanus, and tetanus bacteria or spores enter her body, her life will also be at risk.

Tetanus bacteria or spores grow in dirty cuts. These bacteria can grow if the umbilical cord is cut with an unclean knife or if anything unclean touches the end of the cord. Any tool used to cut the cord should be cleaned, boiled or heated over a flame, and allowed to cool. For the first week after birth, the baby's umbilical stump must be kept clean. No substances should be put on the stump.

All pregnant women should make sure they have been immunized against tetanus. This protects both mothers and newborns.

It is safe for a pregnant woman to be immunized against tetanus. She should be immunized according to this schedule:

First dose:	As soon as she knows she is pregnant.
Second dose:	One month after the first dose, and no later than two weeks before her due date.
Third dose:	Six months to one year after the second dose, or during the next pregnancy.
Fourth dose:	One year after the third dose, or during a subsequent pregnancy.
Fifth dose:	One year after the fourth dose, or during a subsequent pregnancy.

After five properly spaced doses, the mother is protected for life and her children are protected for the first few weeks of life.

5.

A new syringe must be used for every person being immunized. People should demand a new syringe for every vaccination.

SUPPORTING INFORMATION

Sharing syringes and needles, even among family members, can spread life-threatening diseases. A new syringe should be used for every person.

All immunizations in any setting, including emergencies, should be given with auto-disable syringes – syringes that can be used only once.

Parents and other caregivers should demand a new syringe for every vaccination. Health workers must discard the syringes and any other waste by-products safely.

6.

Disease can spread quickly when people are crowded together. All children living in congested conditions, particularly in refugee or disaster situations, should be immunized immediately, especially against measles.

SUPPORTING INFORMATION

Emergencies that make people flee their homes often lead to the spread of communicable diseases. Therefore, all displaced children under 15 years of age should be immediately immunized, especially for measles, at the first point of contact or settlement.

Measles is even more serious when children are malnourished or living in conditions of poor sanitation.

- Diseases like measles spread very quickly. A child with measles needs to be kept away from other children, be examined by a trained health worker and be given a high dose of vitamin A.

- When there is an outbreak of measles in an area, children should be immunized. Neighbouring areas should be alerted and children immunized.

If routine child immunization has been disrupted, a trained health worker should be consulted to complete the immunizations according to national guidelines. If the child's vaccination record is lost and the parents do not remember which vaccines the child has received, it is safe to repeat doses.

7.

The vaccination card of a child (or an adult) should be presented to the health worker before every immunization.

SUPPORTING INFORMATION

It is important to follow the vaccination schedule in accordance with national guidelines. Children should be immunized at the recommended ages and should receive subsequent doses at recommended intervals.

When a child is immunized, the health worker should record the vaccine, which dose it is (first, second, etc.) and the date on an immunization or health card given to the parents or other caregiver. The immunizations should also be recorded and kept at the health clinic. It is important for the parents or other caregiver to keep the immunization card and bring it with them the next time the child is vaccinated. With it, the health worker can record which vaccines the child has received and the date they were given. The health worker can also provide information to the parents or other caregiver on vaccines that are missing or remaining.

Why it is important to share and act on information about
DIARRHOEA

Diarrhoea is the second most common cause of death in young children, after pneumonia. About 4 billion cases of diarrhoea are estimated to occur every year among children under 5. It kills more than 1.5 million children under 5 years of age every year, representing 17 per cent of all deaths in children under 5. Children are more likely than adults to die from diarrhoea because they become dehydrated and malnourished more quickly.

Diarrhoea is caused by germs that are swallowed, especially germs from faeces. This happens most often where there is unsafe disposal of faeces, poor hygiene practices, lack of clean drinking water, or when infants are not breastfed.

Infants who are exclusively breastfed in their first six months and who receive all their immunizations on time are less likely to get diarrhoea. Children with diarrhoea should be given lots of fluids and foods along with a special solution called oral rehydration salts (ORS) and zinc to help reduce the severity of the illness.

Families and communities, with support from governments and non-governmental organizations (NGOs), can do much to raise awareness of (1) what causes diarrhoea, (2) why it is important to treat diarrhoea as soon as it starts, and (3) how to prevent the conditions that cause it.

When everyone works together to reduce diarrhoea, children's right to life, survival, health and development can be better assured.

KEY MESSAGES:
What every family and community
has a right to know about

DIARRHOEA

1. Diarrhoea kills children by draining liquid from the body, which dehydrates the child. As soon as diarrhoea starts, it is essential to give the child extra fluids along with regular foods and fluids.

2. A child's life is in danger if she or he has several watery stools within an hour or if there is blood in the stool. Immediate help from a trained health worker is needed.

3. Exclusive breastfeeding for the first six months of life and continued breastfeeding after six months can reduce the risks associated with diarrhoea. Immunization against rotavirus (where recommended and available) reduces deaths from diarrhoea caused by this virus. Vitamin A and zinc supplementation can reduce the risk of diarrhoea.

4. A child with diarrhoea needs to continue eating regularly. While recovering, she or he needs to be offered more food than usual to replenish the energy and nourishment lost due to the illness.

5. A child with diarrhoea should receive oral rehydration salts (ORS) solution and a daily zinc supplement for 10–14 days. Diarrhoea medicines are generally ineffective and can be harmful.

6. To prevent diarrhoea, all faeces, including those of infants and young children, should be disposed of in a latrine or toilet or buried.

7. Good hygiene practices and use of safe drinking water protect against diarrhoea. Hands should be thoroughly washed with soap and water or a substitute, such as ash and water, after defecating and after contact with faeces, and before touching or preparing food or feeding children.

KEY MESSAGE

1. Diarrhoea kills children by draining liquid from the body, which dehydrates the child. As soon as diarrhoea starts, it is essential to give the child extra fluids along with regular foods and fluids.

SUPPORTING INFORMATION

A child has diarrhoea when she or he passes three or more watery stools a day. The more numerous the watery stools, the more dangerous the diarrhoea.

Some people think that drinking liquids makes diarrhoea worse. *This is not true.* A child with diarrhoea should be given drinks, including breastmilk, as often as possible. Drinking lots of liquids helps to replace the fluids lost during diarrhoea.

Recommended drinks for a child with diarrhoea include:

- breastmilk (mothers should breastfeed more often than usual)
- oral rehydration salts (ORS) mixed with the proper amount of clean water (*refer to the box on ORS after Message 5*)
- soups
- rice water
- fresh fruit juices
- coconut water

clean water from a safe source. If there is a possibility the water is not clean and safe to drink, it should be purified by boiling, filtering, adding chlorine or disinfecting with sunlight in accordance with information provided by a trained health worker or extension agent.

To avoid dehydration, breastfed children should breastfeed as often as possible. Children who are not breastfeeding should drink the following amounts of liquids every time a watery stool is passed:

- for a child under the age of 2 years: between ¼ and ½ of a large (250-millilitre) cup

- for a child 2 years or older: between ½ and 1 whole large (250-millilitre) cup.

Drinks should be given from a clean cup. A feeding bottle should not be used. It is difficult to clean bottles completely, and unclean bottles can contain germs that cause diarrhoea.

If the child vomits, the caregiver should wait 10 minutes and then begin again to give the drink to the child slowly, small sips at a time.

The child should be given extra liquids in addition to regular foods and drinks until the diarrhoea has stopped.

Diarrhoea usually stops after three or four days. If it lasts longer, parents or other caregivers should seek help from a trained health worker.

KEY MESSAGE

2.

A child's life is in danger if she or he has several watery stools within an hour or if there is blood in the stool. Immediate help from a trained health worker is needed.

SUPPORTING INFORMATION

Parents should immediately seek help from a trained health worker if the child:

- passes several watery stools in an hour

- passes blood in the stool

- vomits frequently

- has a fever

- is extremely thirsty

- does not want to drink

- refuses to eat

- has sunken eyes
- looks weak or is lethargic
- has had diarrhoea for several days.

If the child has *any* of these signs, help from a trained health worker is needed urgently. In the meantime, the child should be given ORS solution and/or other liquids, plus zinc.

If the child passes several watery stools in one hour and vomits, there is cause for alarm – these are possible signs of cholera. Cholera can kill children in a matter of hours. Medical help should be sought *immediately* and the child should continue to receive ORS solution and zinc.

- Cholera can spread throughout the community quickly through contaminated water or food. Cholera usually occurs in situations where there is poor sanitation and overcrowding.

- There are four steps to take to limit the spread of cholera or diarrhoea:

  1. Always wash hands with soap and water or a substitute, such as ash and water, after defecation, after contact with faeces, before touching or preparing food, before eating and before feeding children.

  2. Dispose of all faeces, including those of infants and young children, in a latrine or toilet, or bury them. Disinfect the places touched by the faeces.

  3. Use safe drinking water.

  4. Wash, peel or cook all foods.

Trained health workers and health centres should provide families and communities with clear information on the risks of diarrhoea and cholera and what steps to take when either one occurs.

3.

Exclusive breastfeeding for the first six months of life and continued breastfeeding after six months can reduce the risks associated with diarrhoea. Immunization against rotavirus (where recommended and available) reduces deaths from diarrhoea caused by this virus. Vitamin A and zinc supplementation can reduce the risk of diarrhoea.

SUPPORTING INFORMATION

Breastmilk is the best source of liquid and food for a young child with diarrhoea. It is nutritious and clean and helps fight illness and infections. An infant who is fed only breastmilk in her or his first six months of life is less likely to get diarrhoea during this time.

Breastmilk prevents dehydration and malnutrition and helps replace lost fluids. Mothers are sometimes advised to give less breastmilk if a child has diarrhoea. *This advice is wrong.* Mothers should breastfeed more often than usual when the child has diarrhoea. Fathers should support mothers who are breastfeeding by caring for the sick child and other children in the family, and by helping with household tasks.

Rotavirus causes diarrhoea. Children should be immunized against rotavirus in countries that offer this vaccination.

Vitamin A supplementation, particularly in areas deficient in vitamin A, is an important measure to reduce the risk of diarrhoea. Foods that contain vitamin A include breastmilk, liver, fish, dairy products, orange or yellow fruits and vegetables, and green leafy vegetables.

Including zinc as part of the treatment for diarrhoea for 10–14 days helps to reduce its severity and duration, and also protects the child from future diarrhoea episodes for up to two months. Children over 6 months of age can take 20 milligrams per day of zinc (tablet or syrup). For children under 6 months, 10 milligrams per day (tablet or syrup) is an appropriate amount.

The trained health worker should show the mother, father or other caregiver how to give the child a zinc tablet by dissolving it in a small amount of expressed breastmilk, ORS or clean water in a small cup or spoon. If the child is too young for a tablet, zinc syrup can be used.

KEY MESSAGE

4.

A child with diarrhoea needs to continue eating regularly. While recovering, she or he needs to be offered more food than usual to replenish the energy and nourishment lost due to the illness.

SUPPORTING INFORMATION

A child with diarrhoea loses weight and can quickly become malnourished. A child with diarrhoea needs all the foods and fluids, including breastmilk, she or he can take. Nutritious foods will help the child recover more quickly.

A child with diarrhoea may not want to eat or may vomit, so feeding can be difficult. Breastfeeding should be more frequent. If the child is 6 months of age or older, parents and other caregivers should encourage the child to eat as often as possible, offering small amounts of soft, mashed foods or foods the child likes. These foods should contain a *small* amount of salt. Soft foods are easier to eat and contain more fluid than hard foods.

Recommended foods for a child with diarrhoea are well-mashed mixes of cereals and beans, fish, well-cooked meat, yogurt and fruits. A little oil can be added to cereal and vegetables, about 1 or 2 teaspoons. Foods should be freshly prepared and given to the child five or six times a day.

After the diarrhoea stops, extra feeding is vital for a full recovery. At this time, the child needs to be given more food than usual, including breastmilk, to help replenish the energy and nourishment lost due to the diarrhoea.

A child is not fully recovered from diarrhoea until she or he is at least the same weight as when the illness began.

KEY MESSAGE

5.

A child with diarrhoea should receive oral rehydration salts (ORS) solution and a daily zinc supplement for 10–14 days. Diarrhoea medicines are generally ineffective and can be harmful.

SUPPORTING INFORMATION

Diarrhoea usually cures itself in three to four days with rehydration (drinking a lot of liquids). The real danger is the loss of liquid and nutrients from the child's body, which can cause dehydration and malnutrition.

A child with diarrhoea should never be given any tablets, antibiotics or other medicines unless prescribed by a trained health worker.

The best treatment for diarrhoea is to (1) drink lots of liquids and oral rehydration salts (ORS), properly mixed with clean water from a safe source, and (2) take zinc tablets or syrup for 10–14 days.

ORS Solution

A special drink for diarrhoea

DIARRHOEA

What is ORS?	ORS (oral rehydration salts) is a special combination of dry salts that is mixed with safe water. It can help replace the fluids lost due to diarrhoea.
When should ORS be used?	When a child has three or more loose stools in a day, begin to give ORS. In addition, for 10–14 days, give children over 6 months of age 20 milligrams of zinc per day (tablet or syrup); give children under 6 months of age 10 milligrams per day (tablet or syrup).
Where can ORS be obtained?	In most countries, ORS packets are available from health centres, pharmacies, markets and shops.
How is the ORS drink prepared?	1. Put the contents of the ORS packet in a clean container. Check the packet for directions and add the correct amount of clean water. Too little water could make the diarrhoea worse. 2. Add water only. Do not add ORS to milk, soup, fruit juice or soft drinks. Do not add sugar. 3. Stir well, and feed it to the child from a clean cup. Do not use a bottle.
How much ORS drink to give?	Encourage the child to drink as much as possible. A child under the age of 2 years needs at least ¼ to ½ of a large (250-millilitre) cup of the ORS drink after each watery stool. A child aged 2 years or older needs at least ½ to 1 whole large (250-millilitre) cup of the ORS drink after each watery stool.
What if ORS is not available?	Give the child a drink made with 6 level teaspoons of sugar and ½ level teaspoon of salt dissolved in 1 litre of clean water. Be very careful to mix the correct amounts. Too much sugar can make the diarrhoea worse. Too much salt can be extremely harmful to the child. Making the mixture a little too diluted (with more than 1 litre of clean water) is not harmful.

Diarrhoea usually stops in three or four days.
If it does not stop, consult a trained health worker.

6.

To prevent diarrhoea, all faeces, including those of infants and young children, should be disposed of in a latrine or toilet or buried.

Children and adults can swallow germs that cause diarrhoea if faeces come in contact with drinking water, food, hands, utensils or food preparation surfaces.

Flies that settle on faeces and then on food also transmit the germs that cause diarrhoea. To keep away flies and prevent the spread of germs, (1) dispose of faeces safely in a latrine or toilet, (2) keep the latrine or toilet clean, and (3) cover food and drinking water.

All faeces, even those of infants and young children, carry germs and are dangerous. If children defecate without using the latrine or toilet, their faeces should be cleaned up immediately and disposed of in the latrine or toilet or buried. Afterwards, hands should always be washed with soap and water. If soap is not available, ash and water can be used as a substitute. Men and boys can help women and girls in disposing of the faeces.

If there is no toilet or latrine, adults and children should defecate away from houses, paths, water supplies and places where children play. Faeces should then be buried under a layer of soil. Human and animal faeces should be kept away from water sources.

In communities without toilets or latrines, the community should consider joining together to build such facilities. Households can be encouraged to build their own.

7.

Good hygiene practices and use of safe drinking water protect against diarrhoea. Hands should be thoroughly washed with soap and water or a substitute, such as ash and water, after defecating and after contact with faeces, and before touching or preparing food or feeding children.

SUPPORTING INFORMATION

Hands should always be washed with soap and water or a substitute, such as ash and water, after defecating, after helping children use the toilet or latrine, after cleaning the baby's bottom, after disposing of refuse, and immediately before feeding children, handling food or eating.

Young children frequently put their hands in their mouths. So it is important to keep the household area clean and to teach children to wash their hands properly and frequently, especially after defecating and before eating.

Using safe drinking water and keeping it clean and free of germs helps to reduce diarrhoea.

Other hygiene measures that can help to prevent diarrhoea include:

- peel fruit and vegetables or wash them thoroughly with clean water, especially if young children eat them raw

- prepare and thoroughly cook food just before eating (Food left standing can collect germs that can cause diarrhoea. After two hours, cooked foods are not safe unless they are kept very hot or very cold.)

- bury, burn or safely dispose of all food refuse to stop flies from spreading disease.

Why it is important to share and act on information about
COUGHS, COLDS AND MORE SERIOUS ILLNESSES

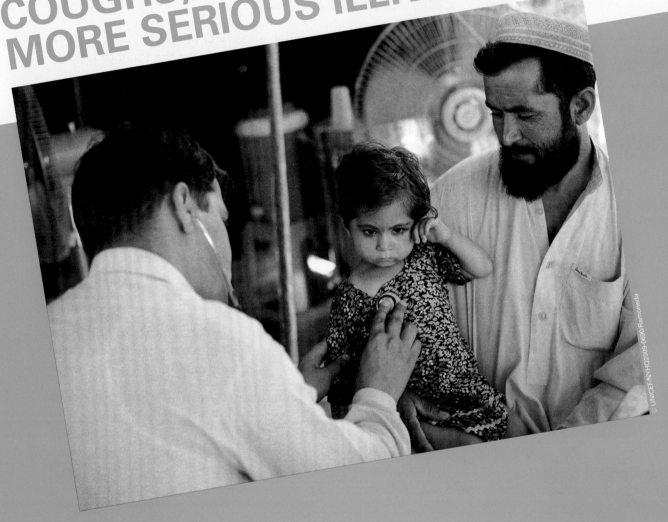

Coughs, colds, sore throats and runny noses are common in the lives of children. Usually they are no cause for alarm.

In some cases, however, coughs are danger signs of more serious illnesses, such as pneumonia or tuberculosis. Pneumonia is the world's leading cause of death in girls and boys under age 5, closely followed by diarrhoea. Around 2 million children die from pneumonia every year. Pneumonia kills more children than AIDS, malaria and measles combined. One out of every five deaths of children under age 5 is caused by this respiratory infection.

All girls and boys have the right to quality health care to make sure that respiratory infections and other illnesses are accurately diagnosed and treated before it is too late.

1. A child with a cough or cold should be kept warm and encouraged to eat and drink as much as possible.

2. Sometimes, coughs are signs of a serious problem. A child who is breathing rapidly or with difficulty might have pneumonia, an infection of the lungs. This is a life-threatening disease. The child needs immediate treatment from a trained health worker, who can also provide a referral to a health facility.

3. Families can help prevent pneumonia by making sure babies are exclusively breastfed for the first six months and that all children are well nourished and fully immunized.

4. A child who has a prolonged cough that persists for more than three weeks needs immediate medical attention. The child may have tuberculosis, an infection in the lungs.

5. Children and pregnant women exposed to smoke from tobacco or cooking fires are particularly at risk of pneumonia or other breathing illnesses.

COUGHS, COLDS AND MORE SERIOUS ILLNESSES

KEY MESSAGE

1.

A child with a cough or cold should be kept warm and encouraged to eat and drink as much as possible.

SUPPORTING INFORMATION

Babies and very young children lose their body heat easily. When they have a cough or cold they should be kept covered and warm.

Children with coughs, colds, runny noses or sore throats who are breathing normally can be treated at home and will recover without medicines. They need to be kept warm, but not overheated, and to be given plenty to eat and drink. Medicines should be used only if prescribed by a trained health worker.

A child with a fever needs careful attention. She or he should be sponged or bathed with cool but not cold water. The child should be kept well hydrated with additional fluids. In areas where malaria is common, the fever could be caused by malaria, which is dangerous to the health and survival of the child. A child with a fever in these areas should be checked by a trained health worker immediately.

The nose of a child with a cough or cold should be cleared often, especially before the child eats or goes to sleep. A moist atmosphere can make breathing easier. It can help if the child breathes water vapour from a bowl of water that is hot but not boiling. The parent or other caregiver should make certain the water is not too hot and that the child is carefully supervised when breathing the water vapour.

A breastfed child who has a cough or cold may have difficulty breastfeeding. Since breastfeeding helps to fight the illness and is important for the child's growth, the mother should continue to breastfeed often. If a child cannot suckle, the breastmilk can be expressed into a clean cup and the child can then be fed from the cup by the mother, father or other caregiver. Before putting the baby to the breast or feeding the baby breastmilk (or breastmilk substitute) from a cup, it helps to clear the baby's nose if it is blocked with secretions.

Children who are 6 months of age or older should be encouraged to breastfeed, eat and drink frequently. When the illness is over, the child should be given extra nutritious foods every day until she or he is at least the same weight as before the illness.

Coughs and colds spread easily. People with coughs and colds should avoid coughing, sneezing or spitting near children. They should cough or sneeze into their elbow or a tissue and dispose safely of the tissue. This should be followed by hand washing with soap. This helps stop the spread of germs.

2.

Sometimes, coughs are signs of a serious problem. A child who is breathing rapidly or with difficulty might have pneumonia, an infection of the lungs. This is a life-threatening disease. The child needs immediate treatment from a trained health worker, who can also provide a referral to a health facility.

SUPPORTING INFORMATION

Most coughs, colds, fevers, sore throats and runny noses end without requiring medication. But sometimes a cough and a fever are signs of pneumonia, which needs to be treated by a trained health worker.

If a trained health worker provides antibiotics to treat the pneumonia, it is important to follow the instructions and give the child all the medicine for as long as the instructions say, even if the child seems better.

Many children die of pneumonia at home because their parents or other caregivers do not realize the seriousness of the illness and the need for immediate medical care. Millions of child deaths from pneumonia can be prevented if:

- parents and other caregivers know that rapid and difficult breathing is a danger sign, requiring urgent medical help

- parents and other caregivers know where to get medical help

- medical help and appropriate and low-cost antibiotics are readily available.

The child should be taken immediately to a trained health worker or clinic if any of the following symptoms are present:

- the child is breathing much more quickly than usual: from birth to 59 days – 60 breaths a minute; 2 months to 12 months – 50 breaths a minute or more; over 12 months to 5 years – 40 breaths a minute or more

- the child is breathing with difficulty or gasping for air
- the lower part of the chest sucks in when the child breathes in, or it looks as though the stomach is moving up and down
- the child has had a cough for more than three weeks
- the child is unable to breastfeed or drink
- the child vomits frequently.

Health-care providers have a responsibility to provide parents and other caregivers with this information on the health risks for a child with pneumonia and the preventive steps and treatments to take.

3.

Families can help prevent pneumonia by making sure babies are exclusively breastfed for the first six months and that all children are well nourished and fully immunized.

SUPPORTING INFORMATION

Breastfeeding helps to protect babies from pneumonia and other illnesses. It is important to give breastmilk *alone* for the first six months of a baby's life.

After 6 months of age, a child should eat a variety of healthy foods, and continue to be breastfed, to ensure that she or he gets the nutrients necessary to stay healthy and be less susceptible to respiratory infections and other illnesses. Some examples of healthy foods include fruits and vegetables (including green leafy vegetables), liver, red palm oil, dairy products, fish and eggs.

Safe water and good hygiene practices help to reduce the number of respiratory infections and other illnesses, such as diarrhoea. These practices include washing vegetables and fruits, keeping food preparation surfaces clean, and washing hands with soap and water or with a substitute, such as ash and water.

Every child should complete a recommended series of immunizations. Early protection is critical; the immunizations in the first year and into the second year are especially important. The child will then be protected against measles, pertussis (whooping cough), tuberculosis and other respiratory illnesses, which can lead to pneumonia.

Parents and other caregivers should ensure that both girls and boys are equally provided with a varied and healthy diet and all immunizations. Health workers can provide parents and other caregivers with information on diets, hygiene and immunizations and how they protect against pneumonia and other illnesses.

4.

A child who has a prolonged cough that persists for more than three weeks needs immediate medical attention. The child may have tuberculosis, an infection in the lungs.

SUPPORTING INFORMATION

Tuberculosis is a serious disease that can kill a child or permanently damage the lungs. Families and caregivers can help prevent tuberculosis if they ensure that children:

- are fully immunized – BCG immunization offers some protection against some forms of tuberculosis

- are kept away from anyone who has tuberculosis or has a cough with blood in the sputum.

If a trained health worker provides special medicine for tuberculosis, it is important to give the child all the medicine according to the instructions. It must be given for as long as specified, even if the child seems better. If not, the child could build up resistance to the medicine, reducing its effectiveness the next time it is needed.

5.

Children and pregnant women exposed to smoke from tobacco or cooking fires are particularly at risk of pneumonia or other breathing illnesses.

SUPPORTING INFORMATION

Children are more likely to get pneumonia and other breathing illnesses if they live in an environment with smoke.

Exposure to smoke can harm a child, even before birth. Pregnant women should not smoke or be exposed to smoke. Babies especially should be kept out of smoky kitchens and away from cooking fires.

Tobacco use generally begins during adolescence. Adolescents are more likely to start smoking if (1) the adults around them smoke, (2) tobacco advertising and promotion are common, and (3) tobacco products are cheap and easily accessible. Adolescents should be encouraged to avoid smoking and caution their friends about its dangers.

Second-hand smoke is particularly harmful to young children. It stays in the air for hours after cigarettes, pipes or cigars have been put out. Non-smokers who inhale this smoke are more vulnerable to respiratory infections, asthma and cancer.

Parents and other caregivers need to be aware of the detrimental effects of second-hand smoke and take responsibility to refrain from smoking around children. Governments and communities can work together to inform the public of the harmful effects of smoky environments and second-hand smoke on children.

Why it is important to share and act on information about
HYGIENE

Young children are more vulnerable than any other age group to the ill effects of unsafe water, poor sanitation and lack of hygiene. These contribute to 88 per cent of deaths from diarrhoeal diseases. Children under 5 years old account for nearly 90 per cent of deaths from diarrhoea.

The simple habit of handwashing with soap is estimated to reduce the incidence of diarrhoea by nearly half. It also greatly reduces the risk of respiratory infections such as pneumonia and other diseases, including eye infections, especially trachoma.

Parents and caregivers should wash their hands with soap and water at these critical moments: (1) after cleaning the infant or young child who has defecated, (2) after helping the child use the toilet or latrine, (3) after going to the latrine or toilet themselves, (4) before touching food and feeding young children, and (5) after dealing with refuse.

Parents and caregivers need to help children develop the habit of washing their hands with soap before eating and after using the latrine or toilet. Where soap is not available hands can be washed with ash and water. Animal and human faeces should be kept away from houses, paths, water sources and children's play areas.

The use of latrines and toilets together with good hygiene practices – specifically hand washing with soap – are essential public health tools. They protect children and families at little cost and help realize children's right to good health and nutrition.

Everyone in the community needs to work together to build and use toilets or latrines, practise good hygiene, protect water sources, and safely dispose of waste water and refuse.

It is important for governments to support communities by providing information on how to design and build latrines and toilets that all families can afford. In urban areas particularly, government support is also needed for low-cost sanitation and drainage systems, safe drinking water and refuse collection.

HYGIENE

1. All faeces, *including* those of babies and young children, should be disposed of safely. Making sure that all family members use a toilet, latrine or potty (for young children) is the best way to dispose of faeces. Where there is no toilet, faeces should be buried.

2. All family members, including children, need to wash their hands thoroughly with soap and water after any contact with faeces, before touching or preparing food, and before feeding children. Where soap is not available, a substitute, such as ash and water, can be used.

3 Washing the face and hands with soap and water every day helps to prevent eye infections. In some parts of the world, eye infections can lead to trachoma, which can cause blindness.

4. All water that people drink and use should come from a safe source or be purified. Containers for carrying and storing water need to be kept clean inside and outside and covered to keep the water clean. Where necessary, home-based water treatment, such as boiling, filtering, adding chlorine or disinfecting with sunlight, should be used to purify the water.

5. Raw or leftover cooked food can be dangerous. Raw food should be washed or cooked. Cooked food should be eaten without delay or thoroughly reheated before eating.

6. Food, utensils and preparation surfaces should be kept clean and away from animals. Food should be stored in covered containers.

7. Safe disposal of all household refuse helps to keep the living environment clean and healthy. This helps prevent illness.

8. Hygiene is very important during menstruation. Clean and dry feminine hygiene products should be available to girls and women. A clean, private space should be provided to allow them to clean themselves and wash and dry their cloths. Sanitary napkins need to be disposed of carefully with other refuse or burned.

HYGIENE

1.

All faeces, *including* those of babies and young children, should be disposed of safely. Making sure that all family members use a toilet, latrine or potty (for young children) is the best way to dispose of faeces. Where there is no toilet, faeces should be buried.

SUPPORTING INFORMATION

Many illnesses, especially diarrhoea, come from germs found in human faeces. If the germs get into water or onto food, hands, utensils or surfaces used for preparing and serving food, they can be swallowed and cause illness. Safe disposal of all faeces – both human and animal – is the single most important action to prevent the spread of germs by people or flies. Human faeces need to be put down a toilet or latrine, or buried.

All faeces, *including* those of babies and young children, carry germs and are dangerous. If children defecate without using a toilet or latrine, their faeces should be cleaned up immediately and flushed down the toilet or put down the latrine or buried. Parents' or other caregivers' and children's hands should then be washed with soap and water or a substitute, such as ash and water.

If it is not possible to use a toilet or latrine, everyone should always defecate well away from houses, paths, water sources and places where children play. The faeces should then be buried immediately. Animal faeces also need to be kept away from the houses, paths and areas where children play.

Latrines and toilets need to be cleaned frequently. Latrines should be kept covered and toilets should be flushed. A clean latrine attracts fewer flies. People are more likely to use a clean latrine. Local governments and non-governmental organizations can often advise households and communities on the design, materials and construction for building low-cost sanitary latrines.

In urban areas, the government and communities should work together to determine how to install low-cost latrines or toilets, sanitation and drainage systems, safe drinking water and refuse collection.

KEY MESSAGE

2.

All family members, including children, need to wash their hands thoroughly with soap and water after any contact with faeces, before touching or preparing food, and before feeding children. Where soap is not available, a substitute, such as ash and water, can be used.

SUPPORTING INFORMATION

Washing the hands with soap and water removes germs. Rinsing the fingers with water is not enough – both hands need to be rubbed together with soap and water, and then rinsed with water. This helps to stop germs and dirt from getting onto food or into the mouth. Washing hands can also prevent infection with worms. Soap and water should be placed conveniently near the latrine or toilet. Where soap is not available, ash and water can be used.

- It is especially important to wash the hands with soap after defecating and after cleaning the bottom of a baby or child who has just defecated. It is also important to wash hands after handling animals and raw foods.

- Hands should always be washed before preparing, serving or eating food, and before feeding children. Children should be taught to wash both hands rubbed together with soap after defecating and before eating to help protect them from illness.

Children often put their hands into their mouths, so it is important to wash their hands often, especially after they have been playing in dirt or with animals. Washing a child's body regularly is also important to avoid skin infections.

Children are easily infected with worms, which deplete the body's nutrients. Worms and their eggs can be found in human and animal faeces and urine, in surface water and soil, and in poorly cooked meat.

- Children should not play near the latrine, toilet or defecation areas. Shoes or sandals should be worn near latrines to prevent worms from entering the body through the skin of the feet.

● Children living in areas where worms are common should be treated two to three times per year with a recommended deworming medication.

Washing hands with soap and water after handling poultry or poultry products, after touching eggs and raw meat, and after cleaning the place where poultry is kept can also help prevent the spread of germs and avian influenza (bird flu).

KEY MESSAGE

3.

Washing the face and hands with soap and water every day helps to prevent eye infections. In some parts of the world, eye infections can lead to trachoma, which can cause blindness.

SUPPORTING INFORMATION

Flies carry germs. A dirty face attracts flies, spreading the germs from person to person. If the eyes become sore or infected, vision may be impaired or lost. Eyes must be kept clean and healthy.

If the eyes are healthy, the white part is clear, the eyes are moist and shiny, and vision is sharp. If the eyes are extremely dry or very red and sore, if there is a discharge or if there is difficulty seeing, the child should be examined by a trained health worker as soon as possible.

KEY MESSAGE

4.

All water that people drink and use should come from a safe source or be purified. Containers for carrying and storing water need to be kept clean inside and outside and covered to keep the water clean. Where necessary, home-based water treatment, such as boiling, filtering, adding chlorine or disinfecting with sunlight, should be used to purify the water.

SUPPORTING INFORMATION

Families have fewer illnesses when they have an adequate supply of safe water and know how to keep it clean and free from germs. If the water is not clean it can be purified using low-cost solutions at home. It can be (1) boiled, (2) cleaned through a filter, (3) purified with chlorine or (4) disinfected with sunlight or other simple measures.[10] The trained health worker or extension agent should have information on home treatments that are available locally.

Safe water sources include properly constructed and maintained piped systems, public standpipes, boreholes, pond sand filters, protected dug wells, protected springs and rainwater collection. Water from unsafe sources –

---

10 Other home-based water treatment measures include keeping water in clear plastic bottles in strong sunlight for six hours or using combination flocculation-disinfection sachets that clean and disinfect the water.

rivers, dams, lakes, ponds, streams, canals, irrigation channels, unprotected wells and springs – is best avoided. If necessary it can be made safer by the home-based water treatment methods referred to above. Water should be safely stored in a covered container that is clean on the inside and outside.

Families and communities can protect their water supply by:

- lining and covering open wells, installing a handpump and protecting the immediate area from animals and vandalism

- protecting a spring with a spring box

- disposing of faeces and waste water (especially from latrines and household cleaning) well away from any water source used for cooking, drinking or washing

- building latrines at least 15 metres away and downhill from a water source

- always keeping jerry-cans, buckets, pitchers, ropes and jars used to collect and store water as clean as possible by storing them in a clean place, off the ground and away from animals

- keeping all animals away from drinking water sources and family living areas

- avoiding the use of pesticides or chemicals anywhere near a water source.

Families can keep water clean in the home by:

- storing drinking water in a clean, covered container

- washing hands regularly – including before handling stored clean water

- taking water out of the container with a clean ladle or cup

- having a tap on the water container

- not allowing anyone to put their fingers or hands into the container or to drink directly from it

- keeping all animals away from stored water.

If there is uncertainty about the safety of the drinking water, local authorities should be consulted.

5.

Raw or leftover cooked food can be dangerous. Raw food should be washed or cooked. Cooked food should be eaten without delay or thoroughly reheated before eating.

Cooking food thoroughly kills germs. Food, especially meat and poultry, should be cooked all the way through.

Germs grow quickly in warm food. Food should be eaten as soon as possible after cooking so it does not have time to collect germs.

- If food has to be kept for more than two hours, it should be kept either very hot or very cool.

- If cooked food is saved for another meal, it should be covered to keep off flies and insects and then thoroughly reheated before being eaten.

- Yogurt and sour porridge are good to use in the preparation of meals because their acid prevents the growth of germs.

Raw food, especially poultry and seafood, usually contains germs. Cooked food can collect germs if it touches raw food, and these germs can breed in the cooked food in a few hours. Raw and cooked foods should always be kept separate. Knives, chopping boards and surfaces should always be cleaned with soap and water after preparing raw food.

- Special care should be taken in preparing food for infants and small children. Their food should be freshly made and eaten immediately, not left standing.

- Breastmilk is the safest (and most nutritious) milk for infants and young children. Expressed breastmilk can be stored at room temperature for up to eight hours in a clean, covered container. If older children are given animal milk it should be freshly boiled or pasteurized (a special way of heating milk to destroy harmful bacteria).

- All poultry and poultry products should be cooked the whole way through to prevent the spread of avian influenza (bird flu).

- Fruit and vegetables should be peeled or washed thoroughly with clean water, especially if they are to be eaten raw by young children. Fruits and vegetables are often treated with chemicals such as pesticides and herbicides, which can be harmful.

- Hands should be washed with soap and water after handling raw foods.

6.

Food, utensils and preparation surfaces should be kept clean and away from animals. Food should be stored in covered containers.

SUPPORTING INFORMATION

Germs on food can be swallowed and cause illness. To protect food from germs:

- keep food preparation surfaces clean

- keep knives, cooking utensils, pots and plates clean and covered

- wash cloths used to clean dishes or pans thoroughly every day and dry them in the sun. Wash plates, utensils and pans immediately after eating and put them on a rack to dry

- keep food in clean, covered containers to protect it from insects and animals

- do not use feeding bottles or teats, because they may contain germs that cause diarrhoea. Breastfeed, or feed children from a clean, open cup. If bottles/teats are used, clean them after each use with boiling water.

HYGIENE

7.

Safe disposal of all household refuse helps to keep the living environment clean and healthy. This helps prevent illness.

Germs can be spread by flies, cockroaches, rats and mice, which thrive in garbage such as food scraps and peelings from fruit and vegetables.

If there is no community-wide refuse collection, each family needs a garbage pit where household refuse is buried or burned every day.

Keeping the household and nearby areas clean and free of faeces, refuse and waste water can help prevent disease. Household waste water can be disposed of safely by making a soak pit or a channel to the kitchen garden or to the field.

Chemicals such as pesticides and herbicides can be very dangerous if even small quantities get into the water supply or onto food, hands or feet. Clothes and containers used when handling chemicals should not be washed near a household water source.

Pesticides and other chemicals should not be used around the household or near a water source. Chemicals should not be stored in or near drinking water containers or near food. Never store food or water in pesticide or fertilizer containers.

8.

Hygiene is very important during menstruation. Clean and dry feminine hygiene products should be available to girls and women. A clean, private space should be provided to allow them to clean themselves and wash and dry their cloths. Sanitary napkins need to be disposed of carefully with other refuse or burned.

SUPPORTING INFORMATION

Adolescent and pre-adolescent girls need to be informed about the significance of menstruation in relation to reproduction and the importance of menstrual hygiene. They need information on how to care for and clean themselves when they are menstruating. Boys should also learn about menstruation and be aware of girls' particular hygiene needs.

Hygienic menstruation practices among adolescent girls and women should be promoted and supported.

- Clean and dry feminine hygiene products such as cloths or napkins should be available. Where cloths are used it is important that they are regularly washed with soap and water and dried fully in the sun before the next use. Damp cloths can carry germs that can lead to infections. Used sanitary napkins should be disposed of in a refuse pit or collected and burned.

- Water and soap should be provided in a private place (bathing area, latrine) for girls and women to wash during menstruation and for washing their hands after changing their cloth/napkin. Poor menstruation hygiene can lead to fungal infections. Repeated infections can lead to serious reproductive tract infections. These could cause infertility.

- Schools should have separate latrines for girls and boys. The girls' latrine in particular needs access to water and soap so girls can clean themselves. Latrines that are private, clean and safe contribute to keeping girls in school longer, which can delay early marriage and pregnancy.

When girls and women are menstruating, their privacy needs to be respected.

HYGIENE

Why it is important to share and act on information about
MALARIA

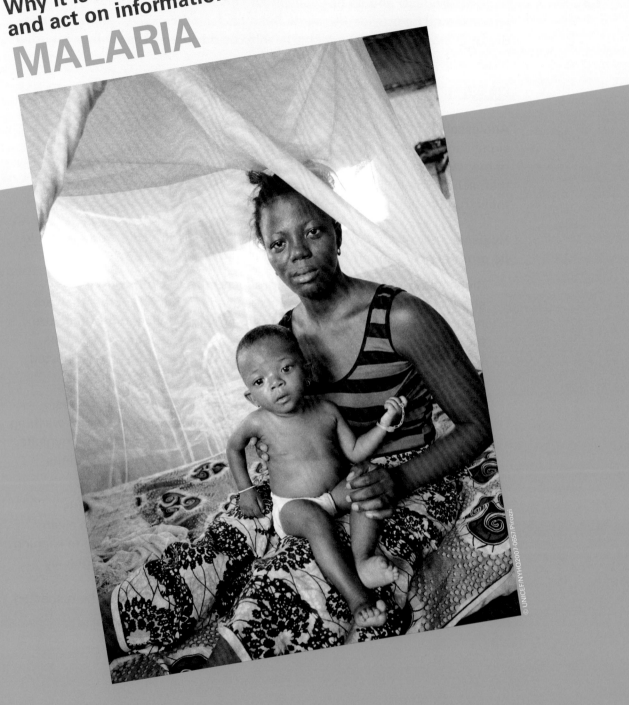

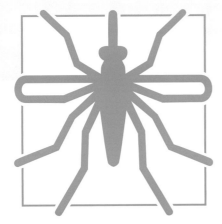

Malaria is a serious disease spread through mosquito bites. The World Health Organization estimates that around 250 million malaria episodes occurred in 2006, resulting in nearly 1 million deaths. About 90 per cent of all malaria deaths occur in sub-Saharan Africa, most among children under age 5.

Malaria is found in many regions of the world. In sub-Saharan Africa, it is a leading cause of death, illness, and poor growth and development among young children. It is estimated that a child dies of malaria every 30 seconds in this area.

Malaria is particularly dangerous for pregnant women. Some 50 million pregnant women are exposed to malaria each year. Malaria during pregnancy contributes to nearly 20 per cent of low-birthweight babies in endemic areas, plus anaemia, stillbirth and even maternal deaths.

Malaria is spread by the bite of an *Anopheles* mosquito. The mosquito transfers the malaria parasite, *Plasmodium*, from person to person. People get very sick with high fevers, diarrhoea, vomiting, headache, chills and flu-like illness. Especially in children, the disease can worsen rapidly, causing coma and death. Children under 5 years old are most susceptible to malaria because they have very little acquired immunity to resist it.

Many lives can be saved by preventing malaria and treating it early. Children and their family members have the right to quality health care for prompt and effective treatment and malaria prevention.

Governments, in collaboration with communities and non-governmental and community-based organizations, can minimize the number of malaria cases. They need to support preventive actions, such as distributing long-lasting insecticide-treated mosquito nets for families to sleep under.

1. Malaria is transmitted through the bites of some mosquitoes. Sleeping under an insecticide-treated mosquito net is the best way to prevent mosquito bites.

2. Wherever malaria is present, children are in danger. A child with a fever should be examined *immediately* by a trained health worker and receive an appropriate antimalarial treatment as soon as possible if diagnosed with malaria. Artemisinin-based combination therapies (ACTs) are recommended by WHO for treatment of *Plasmodium falciparum* malaria. It is the most serious type of malaria and causes nearly all malaria deaths.

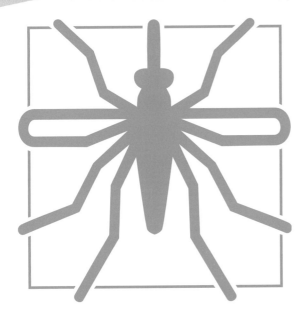

3. Malaria is very dangerous for pregnant women. Wherever malaria is common, they should prevent malaria by taking antimalarial tablets recommended by a trained health worker and by sleeping under an insecticide-treated mosquito net.

4. A child suffering or recovering from malaria needs plenty of liquids and foods.

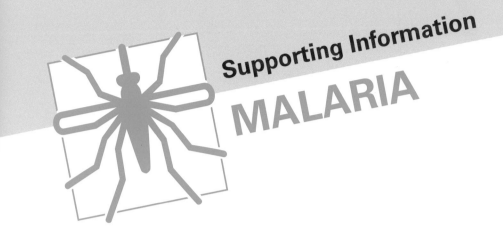

MALARIA

1. Malaria is transmitted through the bites of some mosquitoes. Sleeping under an insecticide-treated mosquito net is the best way to prevent mosquito bites.

SUPPORTING INFORMATION

All members of the community should be protected against mosquito bites, particularly young children and pregnant women. Protection is needed after sunset and before sunrise, when malaria mosquitoes bite.

Long-lasting insecticide-treated mosquito nets last for at least three years and do not require re-treatment with insecticide. These nets are distributed by malaria control programmes and can be obtained through health facilities or during child health days or integrated campaigns. Most mosquito nets are distributed free of charge, especially to pregnant women and young children. They can also be purchased in the marketplace or through social marketing programmes, mainly in urban areas. In the few cases where untreated nets might still be in use, trained health workers can advise on safe insecticides and re-treatment.

Insecticide-treated mosquito nets should be used throughout the year, even when there are fewer mosquitoes, such as during the dry season.

Some countries operate programmes to spray the walls of houses with long-lasting insecticides to kill resting mosquitoes. Communities should cooperate with spray teams to ensure that all houses are sprayed.

In addition to using insecticide-treated mosquito nets, or if mosquito nets are not available or used, other actions can help, but they are not nearly as effective as using mosquito nets:

- putting screens on doors and windows; these are mostly used in urban settings and are not very effective in traditional rural housing

- using mosquito coils; these are used to repel but not kill mosquitoes – they have no lasting effect

- wearing clothing that covers the arms and legs (long sleeves and long trousers or skirts); these can help reduce mosquito bites if worn when malaria mosquitoes are most active – from dusk until dawn.

2.

Wherever malaria is present, children are in danger. A child with a fever should be examined *immediately* by a trained health worker and receive an appropriate antimalarial treatment as soon as possible if diagnosed with malaria. Artemisinin-based combination therapies (ACTs) are recommended by WHO for treatment of *Plasmodium falciparum* malaria. It is the most serious type of malaria and causes nearly all malaria deaths.

SUPPORTING INFORMATION

Malaria should be suspected if anyone in the family has a fever, or if young children refuse to eat or have vomiting, diarrhoea, drowsiness or fits.

A child with a fever believed to be caused by malaria needs immediate antimalarial treatment as recommended by a trained health worker. If possible, the child should be tested with a Rapid Diagnostic Test (RDT) or microscopy (laboratory diagnosis involving the examination of the person's blood under a microscope) to confirm the malaria infection. RDTs are inexpensive and increasingly available.

If a child with a malarial fever is not treated within a day, she or he might die. ACTs are recommended by WHO for treatment of *Plasmodium falciparum* malaria. A trained health worker can advise on what type of ACT treatment is best and how long it should be taken in accordance with national guidelines.

Malaria usually causes a high fever and chills. A child with a high fever should be kept cool for as long as the fever persists by:

- sponging or bathing the child with tepid water (cool, not cold)

- providing treatment with antipyretics (medication that prevents or reduces fever), such as paracetemol or ibuprofen, but not aspirin.

Keeping the fever from going too high is important to prevent convulsions, which could lead to disabilities.

A child with malaria needs to take the *full* course of treatment, even if the fever disappears rapidly. If the treatment is not completed, the malaria could become more severe and difficult to cure. Incomplete treatment regimens can also lead to the development of drug resistance among people in the local area.

If the malaria symptoms continue after treatment, the child should be taken to a health centre or hospital. The problem may be:

- the child is not receiving enough medicine
- the child has an illness other than malaria
- the malaria is resistant to the medicine, and another medicine is needed.

Health-care providers have the responsibility to ensure that parents and caregivers are well informed about ways to prevent malaria and the best practices for caring for a child with malaria.

3.

Malaria is very dangerous for pregnant women. Wherever malaria is common, they should prevent malaria by taking antimalarial tablets recommended by a trained health worker and by sleeping under an insecticide-treated mosquito net.

SUPPORTING INFORMATION

Pregnant women are more likely to suffer from malaria than other women. The disease is more dangerous during pregnancy, especially during the first pregnancy. This is due to changes in a woman's body that lower her previous level of resistance to malaria. Malaria can cause severe anaemia ('thin blood'), miscarriage, premature birth or stillbirth.

Babies born to mothers who have had malaria during pregnancy are often underweight. This makes them more vulnerable to infection or death during their first year.

Women in their first pregnancy in areas where malaria is prevalent often do not show the typical signs of malaria.

As preventive treatment, pregnant women in malarial areas, especially those in their first pregnancy who can be asymptomatic (without symptoms), should take antimalarial tablets in the second and third trimesters as recommended by a trained health worker. The health worker will know which antimalarial tablets are best to take.

It is also very important that pregnant women sleep under insecticide-treated mosquito nets.

Pregnant women with signs and symptoms of *Plasmodium falciparum* malaria must be treated immediately by a trained health worker with quinine in the first trimester and ACTs in the second and third trimesters.

4.

A child suffering or recovering from malaria needs plenty of liquids and food.

SUPPORTING INFORMATION

A girl or boy suffering from malaria should be offered liquids and foods frequently to help prevent dehydration and malnutrition.

Frequent breastfeeding prevents dehydration and helps the child fight infections, including malaria. Children who are breastfeeding and suffering from malaria should be breastfed as often as possible.

Frequent malarial infection can cause anaemia. A child who has had malaria several times should be checked for anaemia.

MALARIA

Why it is important to share and act on information about
HIV

HIV (human immunodeficiency virus) is the virus that causes AIDS (acquired immunodeficiency syndrome). HIV touches the lives of children and families in every country in the world. Over 2 million children under age 15 are living with HIV (infected with HIV). Millions more are affected by HIV (not infected but living in families with infected members). An estimated 17.5 million children have lost one or both parents to AIDS; more than 14 million of these children live in sub-Saharan Africa. (Latest data available, 2007)

HIV is transmitted through (1) unprotected sex with an HIV-infected person; (2) an HIV-infected woman to her baby during pregnancy, childbirth or breastfeeding; and (3) blood from HIV-contaminated syringes, needles or other sharp instruments and from transfusion with HIV-contaminated blood. HIV is not transmitted through casual contact or by other means.

Children are among the most vulnerable to HIV. But they typically receive the fewest services. The disease can progress rapidly in young children. Antiretroviral drugs are used to treat HIV because they restore the immune system and delay progression to AIDS. However, most children infected with HIV do not begin taking these drugs until they are 5–9 years old. *This is too late.* Without antiretroviral treatment, half of all babies born with HIV will die by their second birthday.

Although HIV is still incurable, it is a manageable condition. If infected infants and children are diagnosed early, receive effective treatment and take antiretroviral drugs as prescribed, they have a better chance to grow, learn, develop and have dreams for the future.

Families and communities, especially women and girls, are the first lines of protection and care for children living with or affected by HIV. Families should receive the support they need to provide their children with a nurturing and protective environment. Keeping HIV-positive mothers and fathers alive and healthy is vital for children's growth, development and stability. Without the security of the family, children run a greater risk of being exploited and discriminated against.

Adolescents and young people 15–24 years old accounted for about 45 per cent of all new HIV infections among people aged 15 and older in 2007. HIV is more common among adolescent girls and young women than adolescent boys and young men. Life skills education is critical for children, adolescents and young people so that they acquire the knowledge and skills to make healthy life choices.

Governments, with support from families, communities and non-governmental and faith-based organizations, have a responsibility to ensure people's right to information on HIV prevention, treatment and care. They also have the responsibility to ensure the rights of children living with or affected by HIV to protection, care and support. It is important that children, families and communities help stop the spread of HIV.

KEY MESSAGES:
What every family and community
has a right to know about

HIV

1. HIV (human immunodeficiency virus) is the virus that causes AIDS (acquired immunodeficiency syndrome). It is preventable and treatable, but incurable. People can become infected with HIV through (1) unprotected sexual contact with an HIV-infected person (sex without the use of a male or female condom); (2) transmission from an HIV-infected mother to her child during pregnancy, childbirth or breastfeeding; and (3) blood from HIV-contaminated syringes, needles or other sharp instruments and transfusion with HIV-contaminated blood. It is not transmitted by casual contact or other means.

2. Anyone who wants to know how to prevent HIV or thinks he or she has HIV should contact a health-care provider or an AIDS centre to obtain information on HIV prevention and/or advice on where to receive HIV testing, counselling, care and support.

3. All pregnant women should talk to their health-care providers about HIV. All pregnant women who think they, their partners or family members are infected with HIV, have been exposed to HIV or live in a setting with a generalized HIV epidemic should get an HIV test and counselling to learn how to protect or care for themselves and their children, partners and family members.

4. All children born to HIV-positive mothers or to parents with symptoms, signs or conditions associated with HIV infection should be tested for HIV. If found to be HIV-positive, they should be referred for follow-up care and treatment and given loving care and support.

5. Parents or other caregivers should talk with their daughters and sons about relationships, sex and their vulnerability to HIV infection. Girls and young women are especially vulnerable to HIV infection. Girls and boys need to learn how to avoid, reject or defend themselves against sexual harassment, violence and peer pressure. They need to understand the importance of equality and respect in relationships.

6. Parents, teachers, peer leaders and other role models should provide adolescents with a safe environment and a range of life skills that can help them make healthy choices and practise healthy behaviour.

7. Children and adolescents should actively participate in making and implementing decisions on HIV prevention, care and support that affect them, their families and their communities.

8. Families affected by HIV may need income support and social welfare services to help them take care of sick family members and children. Families should be guided and assisted in accessing these services.

9. No child or adult living with or affected by HIV should ever be stigmatized or discriminated against. Parents, teachers and leaders have a key role to play in HIV education and prevention and in reducing fear, stigma and discrimination.

10. All people living with HIV should know their rights.

HIV

KEY MESSAGE

1. HIV (human immunodeficiency virus) is the virus that causes AIDS (acquired immunodeficiency syndrome). It is preventable and treatable, but incurable. People can become infected with HIV through (1) unprotected sexual contact with an HIV-infected person (sex without the use of a male or female condom); (2) transmission from an HIV-infected mother to her child during pregnancy, childbirth or breastfeeding; and (3) blood from HIV-contaminated syringes, needles or other sharp instruments and transfusion with HIV-contaminated blood. It is not transmitted by casual contact or other means.

SUPPORTING INFORMATION

People infected with HIV usually live for years without any signs of the disease. They may look and feel healthy, but they can still pass on the virus to others. Timely initiation of antiretroviral therapy (ART), a group of medicines used to treat HIV, allows a person to handle HIV as a chronic disease and lead a relatively healthy life.

AIDS is the late stage of HIV infection. People who have AIDS grow weaker because their bodies lose the ability to fight off illnesses. In adults not receiving antiretroviral treatment, AIDS develops 7–10 years after HIV infection, on average. In young children it usually develops much faster. There is no cure for AIDS, but new medicines can help people with AIDS live longer.

In most cases, HIV is passed from one person to another through unprotected sexual intercourse, during which the semen, vaginal fluid or blood of an infected person passes into the body of another person.

HIV can also pass from one person to another through the use of non-sterile, HIV-contaminated needles and syringes (most often among drug users sharing needles and syringes), razor blades, knives or other instruments for injecting, cutting or piercing the body.

People may also become infected by HIV through transfusions of infected blood. All blood for transfusions should be screened for HIV.

HIV is passed to infants and young children primarily from the mother during pregnancy or childbirth or through breastfeeding.

It is not possible to get HIV from working, socializing or living side by side with HIV-positive people. Touching those who are infected with HIV, hugging, shaking hands, coughing and sneezing will not spread the disease. HIV cannot be transmitted through toilet seats, telephones, plates, cups, eating utensils, towels, bed linen, swimming pools or public baths. HIV is not spread by mosquitoes or other insects.

KEY MESSAGE

2.

Anyone who wants to know how to prevent HIV or thinks he or she has HIV should contact a health-care provider or an AIDS centre to obtain information on HIV prevention and/or advice on where to receive HIV testing, counselling, care and support.

SUPPORTING INFORMATION

Information on HIV and on services and education to learn how to prevent or reduce the risk of infection is increasingly available in almost every country. Information can be found at health centres, fixed and mobile HIV care units, testing and counselling centres, youth centres and in many schools. Information is also available through the internet and other media.

HIV testing and counselling can help in early detection of infection. It can enable those who are infected to:

- get the support services they need

- manage other infections they might have

- learn about living with HIV

- learn how to avoid infecting others.

Anyone who thinks that he or she might be infected with HIV should contact a health-care provider or an AIDS centre to receive confidential testing and counselling. Anyone who lives in an area where HIV is prevalent and has had unprotected sex should be encouraged to be tested and counselled.

Voluntary HIV testing and counselling can help people make informed choices about their health and their sexual behaviour. It can help couples decide whether or not to have children. If one partner has HIV there is a risk the other partner can become infected while trying to conceive. If a couple is expecting a baby, testing and counselling can help them make decisions regarding the health of their baby.

Counselling and testing can also help those not infected to remain uninfected through education about ways to avoid risk, including safer sex choices.

There are many types of HIV tests. It is important to talk to a professional to learn about the type of test being used and its accuracy.

If the result of an HIV test is negative, this means the person tested is not infected or it is too early to detect the virus. In adults, the HIV blood test may not detect infection for up to six weeks after exposure. Depending on the test, detection in babies may take up to 18 months after birth. However, early infant diagnosis (EID) can be conducted as early as six weeks.

Families and communities should insist on and support confidential HIV testing, counselling and information. Confidentiality helps protect children, adolescents and adults from experiencing stigma, discrimination, exclusion and isolation.

Counselling can help to empower women and adolescent girls, promote safer sex and condom use, and help detect and facilitate treatment of sexually transmitted infections – all of which can reduce the chances of HIV infection. If a woman or adolescent girl is diagnosed with HIV and has children or is pregnant, assistance may be required to help her protect, care for and support her children. Community support groups and NGOs often provide assistance.

Increasing access to testing followed by treatment, care and support can help to reduce stigma by demonstrating that HIV is not a 'death sentence' and that many people infected with HIV can lead relatively healthy, happy and productive lives.

3.

All pregnant women should talk to their health-care providers about HIV. All pregnant women who think they, their partners or family members are infected with HIV, have been exposed to HIV or live in a setting with a generalized HIV epidemic should get an HIV test and counselling to learn how to protect or care for themselves and their children, partners and family members.

SUPPORTING INFORMATION

The most effective way to reduce transmission of HIV from the mother to the child is to prevent women from becoming infected with HIV. Access to family planning services and condoms for women and men are critical to prevent HIV transmission.

In many countries, pregnancy is the only time when women seek health services. This provides them an important opportunity to receive an HIV test and counselling whether in high- or low-level epidemic areas. If a woman is found to be HIV-positive, she should have access to counselling, referrals, HIV care and treatment, and other health-care services. Health-care and support services for the mother will help reduce the risk of HIV transmission to the baby.

The HIV-positive woman should be encouraged to have her partner and other children tested and counselled. If any test results are positive, HIV care, treatment, and other prevention and health-care services should be offered.

A pregnant woman infected with HIV can take antiretroviral drugs. This can help improve her own health and also reduce the chances of her child becoming infected.

The risk of transmitting HIV to infants may be reduced *to less than 2 per cent* if pregnant women receive comprehensive counselling, health care and antiretroviral treatment during pregnancy and through the first six months after childbirth. This is often part of a comprehensive programme called Prevention of Mother-to-Child Transmission (PMTCT).

An HIV-positive mother of a newborn should be provided with information and skills to select the best feeding option for her baby. She should receive nutrition and health-care counselling for the newborn and herself and be supported in having her child tested and treated for exposure to HIV. She should be informed that babies born to HIV-positive women who have not taken antiretroviral medicines during pregnancy have about a 1 in 3 chance of being born with HIV. Without intervention, half of the babies infected with HIV die before they are 2 years of age.

A pregnant woman infected with HIV needs to know that:

- taking specific medicines (antiretroviral drugs) during pregnancy can help improve her health and reduce the risk of passing the infection to the infant

- prenatal and post-natal care – visiting a skilled birth attendant for check-ups before and after the birth of the baby and receiving care during pregnancy and childbirth – can help reduce the risk of passing the infection to the infant

- starting HIV-exposed newborns on cotrimoxazole or Bactrim between 4 and 6 weeks of age and continuing it until HIV infection can be definitively ruled out can help prevent 'opportunistic' infections (infections that take advantage of a weakened immune system)

- there are various infant feeding practices, each with advantages and risks.

The mother needs to decide which infant feeding practice is the safest and the most manageable for her circumstances:

- *exclusive* breastfeeding for the first six months of the child's life protects the infant from death due to diarrhoea, pneumonia and malnutrition. There is, however, a risk of HIV infection through the breastmilk. The risk of transmitting HIV to the infant is much lower with exclusive breastfeeding than with mixed feeding (breastmilk and other foods and drinks). The risk can also be reduced by shortening the duration of breastfeeding once a nutritionally adequate and safe diet without breastmilk can be provided to the child.

- feeding the baby a breastmilk substitute (infant formula) *alone* eliminates the risk of transmitting HIV through breastmilk but can greatly increase the risk of dying from infections such as diarrhoea or pneumonia, especially in the first 6 months of life. This is a good option only if the mother has access to clean water and the means to obtain the formula for at least 12 months, and the use of infant formula is acceptable to her and her community.

- breastfeeding beyond 6 months should continue until safe and adequate replacement foods, including infant formula and other milks and foods, are available. Once a nutritionally adequate and safe diet can be provided, all breastfeeding should stop.

- all infants, whether they are receiving breastmilk or breastmilk substitutes, should receive other nutritious foods and drinks from 6 months of age onward to provide the energy and nutrients needed to support their growth and development.

(Refer to Message 6 in the Breastfeeding chapter for more information.)

4.

All children born to HIV-positive mothers or to parents with symptoms, signs or conditions associated with HIV infection should be tested for HIV. If found to be HIV-positive, they should be referred for follow-up care and treatment and given loving care and support.

SUPPORTING INFORMATION

The earlier a child is tested, diagnosed with HIV and started on HIV treatment, the better the chance of his or her survival and living a longer and healthier life.

The health-care provider should recommend HIV testing and counselling as part of standard care to all children, adolescents and adults who exhibit signs, symptoms or medical conditions that could indicate HIV infection or who have been exposed to HIV. HIV testing and counselling should be recommended for all children seen in health services in settings where there is a generalized HIV epidemic.

A child whose mother is known to be HIV-positive should be tested for HIV within six weeks of birth or as soon as possible. Infants have their mother's antibodies for several weeks after birth, and therefore standard antibody tests are not accurate for them. A special polymerase chain reaction (PCR) test is required to tell if an infant has the virus around 6 weeks of age. If positive, the child needs to begin treatment immediately. The health-care provider can help the family set up a feasible and appropriate antiretroviral therapy regimen for the child. The parents should receive counselling and social services.

An important part of HIV care and antiretroviral treatment (ART) for children is the antibiotic cotrimoxazole. It helps prevent 'opportunistic' infections related to HIV, especially PCP (pneumocystis pneumonia). This treatment is called cotrimoxazole preventive therapy, or CPT.

Children with HIV should be given ART in fixed-dose combinations. These can be prescribed by a trained health worker, who can also provide follow-up support. If the child is going to school, the school can also provide support to make sure that the child takes the medicines while at school.

It is critical to encourage children taking ART to keep taking the medicines on the recommended schedule. This will help ensure the treatment remains effective.

Children need a healthy, balanced diet under any circumstances, but when they receive HIV treatment, ensuring proper nutrition is especially important.

HIV or opportunistic infections may cause reduced food intake due to decreased appetite, difficulty swallowing or poor absorption. Therefore, extra attention should be given to the nutrition of children who are HIV-positive to make sure they receive high-quality, easily digestible foods. Without proper nutrition, their growth and development can be hindered. This could lead to more opportunistic infections that further deplete children's energy and increase their nutritional needs.

Once children who are HIV-positive are old enough to understand, they need to be involved in decisions about their medical care and support. They also should be made aware of the importance of prompt care and treatment of infections. This is a critical part of developing their ability to make healthy decisions in the future.

KEY MESSAGE

5.

Parents or other caregivers should talk with their daughters and sons about relationships, sex and their vulnerability to HIV infection. Girls and young women are especially vulnerable to HIV infection. Girls and boys need to learn how to avoid, reject or defend themselves against sexual harassment, violence and peer pressure. They need to understand the importance of equality and respect in relationships.

SUPPORTING INFORMATION

While children need to know the biological facts about sex, they also need to understand that sexual relationships involve caring and responsibility. Discussing and stressing the emotional aspect of a sexual relationship with children can help them make healthy decisions and resist peer pressure as they grow and develop. It is important to talk about sex in a way that fits the child's age and stage of development, and conveys values.

Everyone needs to be aware of the fact that adolescent girls and young women are especially vulnerable to HIV infection. Adolescent girls and young women need support to protect themselves from unwanted and unsafe sex.

In many countries, HIV rates are higher among adolescent girls than adolescent boys.

Adolescent girls are more susceptible to HIV infection because:

- they may not have a choice about when to have sex or whether a condom is used

- their vaginal membranes are thinner than those of mature women and thus susceptible to lesions from sexual activity that can allow HIV infection and other sexually transmitted infections (STIs) to enter

- they sometimes are targeted by and engage in relationships with older men who may be infected

- they are vulnerable to being sexually exploited and trafficked, which puts them in high-risk situations.

Girls and women have the right to refuse unwanted and unprotected sex. They also have the right to learn skills on how to avoid, reject or defend themselves against unwanted sexual advances.

Girls and women need to know what to do and where to go if they have been victims of sexual assault. They should seek the support of a trained health worker or go to a health facility for medical attention and counselling. Health-care providers and social workers should be trained to be understanding of girls and women in these situations. This information also applies to cases involving boys.

To effectively address violence, boys and men need to be actively engaged in finding solutions. Their full engagement with girls and women is needed to work on preventing violence and sexual harassment, resisting peer pressure and achieving gender equality. This should include an understanding of gender stereotypes and inequalities.

Discussions at home, in school and in the community between children and adolescents and their parents, teachers, community leaders and other role models can help develop healthy attitudes and behaviours. They can contribute to:

- respect for girls and women and their rights

- equality in decision-making and relationships

- skills development on how to confront peer pressure, sexual harassment, violence and stereotypes.

KEY MESSAGE

6.

Parents, teachers, peer leaders and other role models should provide adolescents with a safe environment and a range of life skills that can help them make healthy choices and practise healthy behaviour.

SUPPORTING INFORMATION

It is important for children to learn about HIV at an early age. When children become adolescents, they need accurate and full information on making and negotiating healthy life choices. This will help them avoid becoming infected with HIV and other sexually transmitted infections (STIs).

Adolescents need to be supported in learning the life skills that can help them protect themselves in situations where they could be vulnerable to HIV infection. These skills include problem solving, decision-making, goal setting, critical thinking, communication, assertiveness and self-awareness. Adolescents also need skills for coping with stressful or confrontational situations.

Adolescents and young people look to parents, teachers, peer leaders and other role models for guidance. These role models should develop their base of knowledge on HIV so they will know how to communicate about HIV and how to share important life skills.

Adolescents need to know the risks of HIV. They need to understand how it is passed through unprotected sex with an infected person or through the use of contaminated needles or syringes for injecting drugs. They should know about safer practices and the consequences of lifestyle choices. They should also know how HIV is not transmitted so they can reject myths and prevent discrimination against people living with HIV that is based on unfounded fears of contagion.

It is important to know and reduce the risks of getting HIV from unprotected sex:

The risk of getting HIV can be reduced if people do not have sex. If they have sex, correct and consistent use of male or female condoms is important. To reduce risk, people can:

- decrease their number of sex partners
- stay in a mutually faithful relationship with a partner(s) who is not infected
- have safer sex – sex without penetration (where the penis does not enter the vagina, rectum or mouth) or penetrative sex using a condom correctly (as the directions indicate) and consistently (during every act of penetrative sex).

In combination with safer practices, male circumcision reduces the possibility of transmission of HIV infection from female to male.

The more sex partners people have, the greater the risk that one of them will have HIV and pass it on (if they do not use male or female condoms consistently and correctly).

However, anyone can have HIV – it is not restricted to those with many sex partners. People who do not show signs of infection may carry the virus. Testing is the only sure way to tell.

A well-lubricated condom is essential for protection during vaginal or anal intercourse.

- The male condoms that come with lubrication (slippery liquid or gel) are less likely to tear during handling or use. If the condom is not lubricated enough, a water-based lubricant, such as silicone or glycerin, should be added. If such lubricants are not available, saliva can be used (although this can transmit other infections, such as herpes). Lubricants made from oil or petroleum should never be used with a male condom because they can damage the condom. Oil or petroleum lubricants include cooking oil, shortening, mineral oil, baby oil, petroleum jellies and most lotions.

- The female condom is a safe alternative to the male condom. The most commonly used female condom is a soft, loose-fitting sheath that lines the vagina. It has a soft ring at each end. The ring at the closed end is used to put the device inside the vagina; it holds the condom in place during sex. The other ring stays outside the vagina and partly covers the labia. Before sex begins, the woman inserts the female condom with her fingers. Only water-based lubricants should be used with female condoms made of latex, whereas water-based or oil-based lubricants can be used with female condoms made of polyurethane or artificial latex (nitrile).

HIV can be transmitted through oral sex, although available information suggests the risk is minimal as compared to vaginal and anal sex. However, oral sex can transmit STIs which can increase the risk of HIV transmission. In the case of oral-penile sex, a male condom is recommended.

Because most sexually transmitted infections can be spread through genital contact, a condom should be used before genital contact begins.

Drinking alcohol or taking drugs interferes with judgement. Even those who understand the risks of HIV and the importance of safer sex may become careless after drinking or using drugs.

People who have sexually transmitted infections (STIs) are at greater risk of getting HIV and spreading HIV to others:

STIs, including HIV, are infections that are spread through sexual contact. They can be spread through the exchange of body fluids (semen, vaginal fluid or blood) or by contact with the skin of the genital area. STIs are spread more easily if there are lesions such as blisters, abrasions or cuts. STIs often cause lesions, which contribute to spreading the infection.

STIs often cause serious physical suffering and damage.

Any STI, such as gonorrhoea or syphilis, can increase the risk of HIV infection or HIV transmission. Anyone suffering from an STI has a much higher risk of becoming infected with HIV if they have unprotected sexual intercourse with an HIV-infected person.

- People who suspect they have an STI should see a trained health worker promptly to be diagnosed and treated. They should avoid sexual intercourse or practise safer sex (non-penetrative sex or sex using a male or female condom).

- Correct and consistent use of male and female condoms when engaging in sexual intercourse – vaginal, anal or oral – can greatly reduce the spread of most STIs, including HIV.

- People who have an STI should tell their partner(s). Unless both partners are treated for an STI, they will continue infecting each other. Most STIs are curable.

Some STI symptoms:

- A man may have pain while urinating; a discharge from his penis; or sores, blisters, bumps or rashes on the genitals or inside the mouth.

- A woman may have vaginal discharge that has a strange colour or bad smell, pain or itching around the genital area, and pain or bleeding from the vagina during or after intercourse. More severe infections can cause fever, pain in the abdomen and infertility.

- Many STIs in women and some in men produce no noticeable symptoms.

Not every problem in the genital area is an STI. Some infections, such as candidiasis (yeast infection) and urinary tract infections, are not spread by sexual intercourse. But they can cause great discomfort in the genital area.

HIV can be spread by unsterilized, contaminated needles or syringes, most often those used for injecting drugs, and by other instruments:

An unsterilized needle or syringe can pass HIV and other infections, such as hepatitis, from one person to another if contaminated with infected blood. Nothing should be used to pierce a person's skin unless it has been sterilized.

People who inject themselves with drugs or have unprotected sex with injecting drug users are at high risk of becoming infected with HIV. People who inject drugs should always use a clean needle and syringe. They should never use another person's needle or syringe.

Injections should be given only by a trained health worker using an auto-disable syringe (a syringe that can be used only once).

Any kind of cut using an unsterilized object such as a razor or knife can transmit HIV. The cutting instrument must be fully sterilized for each person, including family members, or rinsed with bleach and/or boiling water.

Equipment for dental treatment, tattooing, facial marking, ear or body piercing, and acupuncture is not safe unless the equipment is sterilized for each person. The person performing the procedure should take care to avoid any contact with blood during the procedure.

7.

Children and adolescents should actively participate in making and implementing decisions on HIV prevention, care and support that affect them, their families and their communities.

SUPPORTING INFORMATION

Children, adolescents, youth and families can be powerful agents of change in HIV prevention and education and reducing stigma and discrimination. They need to be a central part of defining and implementing responses to HIV.

Children and young people can raise awareness of HIV and compassion for those living with HIV. They often gain confidence and self-esteem in the process of working with their peers and in their communities.

- Child forums and other events provide opportunities for children and young people to mobilize communities to create supportive and caring environments for children and families living with and affected by HIV.

- Schools and non-formal educational activities can help children form peer-to-peer support groups and children's clubs. These can bring together children who, with support from teachers or community workers, take on responsibility to conduct HIV prevention and life skills education.

Children, young people, parents, other caregivers and families affected by HIV can find support by joining or organizing self-help groups, peer groups and community support groups. These groups can:

- provide a social network that gives members psychological support

- share practical information and help families access social welfare services

- offer opportunities for members to become active in efforts to find innovative ways to address HIV prevention, protection, care and support.

In collaboration with local authorities and governments, non-governmental and faith-based organizations often help support these groups.

When groups join to form a network, they can help to create a movement to raise awareness and understanding of HIV and promote protection, care and support of orphans and vulnerable children and families affected by HIV. Such efforts can help to address the exclusion, stigma and discrimination experienced by those living with or affected by HIV.

8.

Families affected by HIV may need income support and social welfare services to help them take care of sick family members and children. Families should be guided and assisted in accessing these services.

SUPPORTING INFORMATION

Families provide the 'first line' response for protecting, caring for and supporting children infected with or affected by HIV. Families and relatives absorb almost all the costs involved in caring for these children.

Families are generally recognized as the best source of the loving care, protection and support that children need. Mothers, fathers or other primary caregivers infected with HIV need support to live longer. Prolonging their lives and keeping them healthy helps to keep a family together.

The majority of children who have lost one or both parents are living in families that are often stretched economically and in need of support. Caregivers tend to be female, including some who are children themselves and many who are elderly, such as grandmothers.

Partnerships involving the government and community or non-governmental or faith-based organizations can provide support to improve the economic situation of families affected by HIV. Support might include access to microcredit, low-interest bank loans and social grants.

How to access income support, such as social grants, and social welfare services, should be clearly detailed in national guidelines. These should be well communicated, understood and administered at the local level. Information provided by families when applying for social grants and services should be kept confidential.

As part of the social welfare services, health-care providers should make sure that HIV-positive children and adults from the same family can obtain treatment and support in the same health facility. This helps conserve the family's time, energy and resources.

Social welfare services, with support from community and non-governmental and faith-based organizations, should help parents and other caregivers develop the skills needed to care for children infected with or affected by HIV.

If the child is HIV-positive, the caregivers need help to:

- learn about the HIV infection

- know how to care for and support the child, including ensuring adherence to an ART regimen

- reduce their fear of contracting HIV from the child

- know how to protect themselves when caring for the child

- understand and respond to the emotional needs of the child.

A child who has lost a parent, other caregiver or sibling because of AIDS needs psychosocial support from his or her family and possibly counselling to work through the trauma and grief. A parent or other caregiver may need support to understand the stages of a child's grief relative to his or her age, as well as appropriate psychosocial responses.

Parents living with HIV should make sure that each of their children has a birth certificate. Parents should make a will to establish 1) who will be the guardians of their children and 2) if they have money land or livestock how these assets will be distributed. If the children are old enough to understand, they should be involved in these deliberations with their parents.

KEY MESSAGE

9.

No child or adult living with or affected by HIV should ever be stigmatized or discriminated against. Parents, teachers and leaders have a key role to play in HIV education and prevention and in reducing fear, stigma and discrimination.

SUPPORTING INFORMATION

Educating children, families and communities about HIV is an essential way to help reduce fear, stigma and discrimination against the child and his or her family living with or affected by HIV, as well as the child's own fears and self-stigma.

Children, parents, other family members, teachers, community and faith-based organizations, local leaders and authorities, and the government have a significant role to play in HIV education and prevention and in reducing fear, isolation, stigma and discrimination.

HIV prevention and education should include:

- Raising awareness and support for the rights of children and family members living with or affected by HIV

  - Children, adolescents and adults living with or affected by HIV have the same rights as any other person to education, health care, housing and appropriate representation in the media. They should also have access to fair and equal treatment in the justice system.

- Ensuring that all children and young people understand the risks of HIV and know that they cannot get it from ordinary social contact with someone who is infected with HIV

  - Children and young people need to be informed that HIV has no vaccination or cure, but that people can lead relatively healthy and productive lives with treatment. It is important that they understand how to prevent HIV infection and how to protect themselves and their loved ones.

- Empowering adolescents and youth to make decisions on when to have or not to have sex and how to negotiate condom use

  - Talking with and listening to young people is very important to understand their situation and how best to provide them with protection, care and support. It can sometimes be awkward for adults to discuss sexual issues with children and adolescents. One way to begin the discussion with school-aged children is to ask them what they have heard about HIV and AIDS. If any of their information is wrong, it provides an opportunity to give them the correct information.

- Stimulating ideas and providing guidance on ways children, adolescents and youth can show their compassion and friendship with children and families they know who are living with or affected by HIV.

KEY MESSAGE

10.

All people living with HIV should know their rights.

SUPPORTING INFORMATION

Governments have a responsibility to ensure protection of the rights of children and their family members infected with or affected by HIV and to collaborate with families, communities and non-governmental and faith-based organizations.

Where AIDS intersects with extreme poverty, conflict and large families, comprehensive support to all orphans and vulnerable children is wise and cost-effective. Children infected with or affected by HIV should be fully included in such strategies and their rights should be protected – including rights to privacy, confidentiality and non-discrimination.

Many children live in difficult circumstances without full protection of their rights. They may be infected with HIV or at risk of exposure. They may live on the streets, in orphanages or in extreme poverty or exploitative situations. These children have the right to live in a family. Their families may need help reuniting and/or staying together. All these children should receive support to go to school and/or get vocational training. They should also receive support to access health and nutritional care as well as legal and social welfare services. They have a right to these services.

Local authorities and non-governmental, faith-based and community-based organizations can help mothers, fathers, other caregivers, children and adolescents living with or affected by HIV know their rights and understand how to advocate for them in relation to the country's judicial and administrative systems, as well as with government authorities responsible for policies, programmes and services.

Why it is important to share and act on information about
CHILD PROTECTION

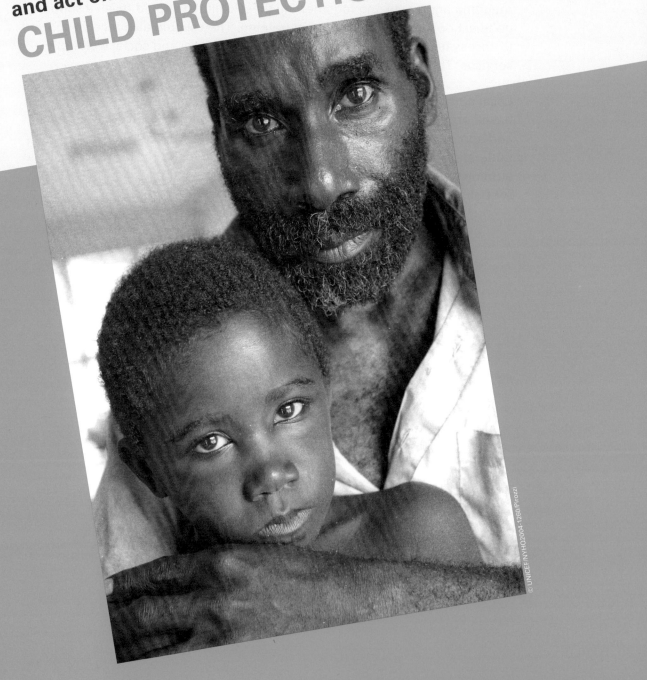

All children have the right to protection. They have the right to survive, to be safe, to belong, to be heard, to receive adequate care and to grow up in a protective environment.

A family is the first line of protection for children. Parents or other caregivers are responsible for building a protective and loving home environment. Schools and communities are responsible for building a safe and child-friendly environment outside the child's home. In the family, school and community, children should be fully protected so they can survive, grow, learn and develop to their fullest potential.

Millions of children are not fully protected. Many of them deal with violence, abuse, neglect, exploitation, exclusion and/or discrimination every day. Such violations limit their chances of surviving, growing, developing and pursuing their dreams.

Any child can be vulnerable to violations in many places, including the home. The actual number of children experiencing violations is not easy to determine. This type of data is hard to collect and is not updated frequently. However, it is estimated that:

- about 150 million girls and 73 million boys under 18 experienced forced sexual intercourse and other forms of sexual violence and exploitation during 2002

- 150 million children aged 5–14 are engaged in child labour

- millions of children, mostly girls, work as domestic labourers (maids) in private homes

- approximately 1.2 million children are trafficked annually (most recent annual estimate from 2000)

- the births of around 51 million children born in 2007 were not registered

- between 22 per cent and 84 per cent of children 2–14 years old experienced physical punishment in the home in 37 countries surveyed between 2005 and 2007.

Governments, communities, local authorities and non-governmental organizations, including faith-based and community-based organizations, can help ensure that children grow up in a family environment. They can make sure that schools and communities protect all children and prevent child maltreatment. They can protect girls and boys from violations such as abuse, sexual exploitation, trafficking and work in hazardous conditions, as well as harmful practices, including child marriage.

Girls and boys should be encouraged and supported to speak up for children's rights and to take an active role in their own protection against abuse, violence, exploitation and discrimination.

KEY MESSAGES:
What every family and community
has a right to know about

CHILD PROTECTION

1. Every child should have the opportunity to grow up in a family. If a family is unable to care for the child, steps should be taken by the authorities to address the reasons and make every effort to keep the family together.

2. Every child has a right to a name and nationality. Registering a child's birth helps to ensure a child's right to education, health care and legal and social services. Birth registration is a vital step towards protection from abuse and exploitation.

3. Girls and boys must be protected from all forms of violence and abuse. This includes physical, sexual and emotional abuse, neglect and harmful practices such as child marriage and genital mutilation/cutting of girls. Families, communities and authorities are responsible for ensuring this protection.

4. Children must be protected from all work that is hazardous. Work should not prevent them from attending school. Children should never be involved in the worst forms of child labour, such as slavery, forced labour, drug production or trafficking.

5. Girls and boys can be at risk of sexual abuse and exploitation in their home, school, workplace or community. Measures should be taken to prevent sexual abuse and exploitation. Sexually abused and exploited children need immediate help to stop such abuse.

6. Children are vulnerable to trafficking where protection for children is weak or missing. The government, civil society and families are responsible for preventing trafficking, as well as helping children who are victims to reintegrate into their families and communities, if it is in their best interest.

7. Justice for children should be based on child rights. Depriving children of their liberty (incarcerating them) must always be a last resort. Procedures that are sensitive to children should be put in place for children who are victims or witnesses of crime.

8. Income support and social welfare services can help keep families together and children in school and ensure access to health care.

9. All children have a right to age-appropriate information, to be heard and to participate in making decisions that concern them. Fulfilment of this right enables children to take an active role in their own protection against abuse, violence and exploitation, and to become active citizens.

1. Every child should have the opportunity to grow up in a family. If a family is unable to care for the child, steps should be taken by the authorities to address the reasons and make every effort to keep the family together.

SUPPORTING INFORMATION

Children grow best in a loving family environment in which their best interests are always taken into account.

If a child is living without a parent or other caregiver, the authorities should take immediate action to reunite the child with her or his own family or extended family. But if it is determined that reunification is not the best option for the child, another permanent family situation should be sought. Every effort should be made to keep siblings together.

Governments, with the support of civil society, have a responsibility to provide appropriate and well-monitored alternative care for children without families. Options include placement with:

- extended family
- a pre-screened foster family
- a residential facility that is integrated within the community, providing family-like care and supporting regular contact between the child and her or his family with the aim of reunification, if it is in the best interest of the child.

Children should be involved in decisions on their placement in alternative living situations.

Very often children placed in institutions could be raised in a family with the proper social support. While some orphanages are well managed, institutional life can be detrimental to children's development. It typically separates them from family and community life and offers less protection from abuse and exploitation.

Any form of institutional care should be considered a last resort and a temporary solution.

KEY MESSAGE

2. Every child has a right to a name and nationality. Registering a child's birth helps to ensure a child's right to education, health care and legal and social services. Birth registration is a vital step towards protection from abuse and exploitation.

SUPPORTING INFORMATION

Birth registration provides an official record of a child's existence and nationality. It is considered a fundamental human right. A child without a birth certificate can be denied health care, legal services, access to school and the right to vote upon reaching adulthood.

Registering a child's birth is a vital step towards her or his protection. Children under age 5 with a birth certificate are more likely to be immunized and receive health care for childhood illnesses, assuring them a healthy start in life.

Any enforcement of minimum-age legislation depends upon an official record of a child's age. For example, a birth certificate can be used to protect a child from illegal recruitment by armed forces or armed groups, from child marriage or from hazardous forms of work.

Birth registration should be free and accessible for every child. Where it is not, civil society organizations can sometimes assist families in registering their children.

The birth registration process may be supported by social services, such as health care and education. Health centres and hospitals sometimes have civil registrars on site that can provide a child's birth certificate at birth or during a health-care visit. Registration sometimes takes place in early childhood education programmes.

3.

Girls and boys must be protected from all forms of violence and abuse. This includes physical, sexual and emotional abuse, neglect and harmful practices such as child marriage and genital mutilation/cutting of girls. Families, communities and authorities are responsible for ensuring this protection.

SUPPORTING INFORMATION

Girls and boys can encounter different forms of violence, abuse and/or harmful practices in many settings:

In the family and home:

- physical violence
- psychological violence
- sexual violence and abuse
- corporal (physical) punishment
- neglect and abandonment
- child marriage
- harmful traditional practices, such as female genital mutilation/cutting (FGM/C).

In schools and other educational activities:

- corporal punishment
- psychological punishment
- sexual and gender-based violence
- verbal and physical bullying
- fighting.

In care and justice institutions (e.g., orphanages, children's homes and detention facilities):

- physical and psychological violence under the guise of discipline
- neglect
- child-on-child violence
- sexual abuse and violence.

In workplaces:

- physical and psychological punishment
- humiliation
- sexual harassment and abuse.

In the community (among peers, between gangs, by the police and by traffickers):

- physical violence
- armed violence
- sexual violence.

Children who experience or witness violence often remain silent out of fear, shame or stigma. Some accept it as part of life. While some violence is perpetrated by strangers, most is carried out by people children know and should be able to trust and look to for protection. These may include parents, step-parents or a parent's partner, relatives, caregivers, boyfriends and girlfriends, schoolmates, teachers, religious leaders and employers.

All girls and boys can be subjects of abuse. Generally, boys tend to be at greater risk of physical and armed violence and girls face greater risk of neglect and sexual violence and exploitation.

Certain groups of children are particularly vulnerable to violence. These include children with disabilities, children of minority groups, children living or working on the street, children in conflict with the law, and children who are refugees, displaced or migrating.

Babies and young children are sometimes the object of a parent's or other caregiver's anger or frustration, often when children do not stop crying. The caregiver may shake the baby or young child so hard and violently that it causes injury to the child's brain that can lead to permanent injury or death. It is *never* okay to shake a child. Symptoms of violent shaking include irritability, difficulty staying awake, difficulty breathing, shakiness, vomiting, seizures or coma. These symptoms require immediate medical care.

Typically, the focus is on intervention after child maltreatment occurs. Due to the magnitude of the problem, it is critical that communities shift the emphasis to *preventing* child violence, abuse, neglect and harmful practices.

Every community should create and implement a plan of action to eliminate violence against children.

Some key actions may include:

- develop and broadly communicate codes of conduct against all forms of violence in settings where children live, go to school, play and work
- educate parents and caregivers to respect the child's perspective, learn how to use positive and non-violent discipline and not to discipline a child when angry
- support schools to nurture attitudes that reject violence and promote non-violent conflict resolution. This can involve changing classroom management (traditionally based on fear, threats, humiliation and physical punishment) to a child-friendly approach that is non-discriminatory and supports cooperative learning
- sponsor public campaigns to stop corporal punishment, abuse and harmful practices such as child marriage and genital mutilation/cutting
- provide children affected by violence with health and social services to help them reintegrate into their families and communities
- establish safe ways for children to report violence against them, such as telephone hotlines or accessible social protection centres.

4.

Children must be protected from all work that is hazardous. Work should not prevent them from attending school. Children should never be involved in the worst forms of child labour, such as slavery, forced labour, drug production or trafficking.

Children who work often do so to support their families' livelihood so they can eat and have basic necessities. Many children begin working at an early age, as young as 4 years old. In many cases, it is considered normal for children to work long hours before or after school, or to work all day and evening and not attend school at all.

Children can be found working in agriculture, commerce, factories, fishing, markets, housekeeping, childcare, handicrafts, restaurants, garbage dumps and in the streets.

Close to 70 per cent of working children work in agriculture, which can be extremely hazardous. It can involve heavy manual labour, long hours, and the use of pesticides and dangerous tools. Children can be at risk of sexual abuse and exploitation, especially during harvesting season (when they often work extra-long hours) and while working on plantations.

Some children are engaged in the worst forms of child labour, such as child slavery, debt bondage, forced labour, drug production and trafficking. *These are illegal.* Children must be removed immediately from such situations and, if it is in their best interest, reintegrated into their families and communities.

The work children do should not be hazardous to their health or well-being. It should not prevent children from going to school.

The government and local authorities, with support from families and civil society, should develop measures to address harmful child labour situations, such as:

- identifying and communicating to the general public the different forms of harmful child labour found in the community and the forms children might encounter if they migrate

- identifying and removing children from harmful child labour

- helping children removed from harmful child labour who live away from their families to reintegrate into their family and community, if it is in their best interest

- ensuring that all children in the community attend a child-friendly school full-time and receive an education that is of good quality, equal for all children and free from violence

- providing income support and/or social welfare services to families who need them, so they are less reliant on their children's income and can send them to school.

Families need to know the risks involved in sending their children away for work, such as domestic and agricultural work.

Children and adolescents should be well informed about the dangers of leaving home and taking work that might land them in high-risk situations such as prostitution and drug trafficking.

5.

Girls and boys can be at risk of sexual abuse and exploitation in their home, school, workplace or community. Measures should be taken to prevent sexual abuse and exploitation. Sexually abused and exploited children need immediate help to stop such abuse.

SUPPORTING INFORMATION

Children need to be protected from all forms of sexual exploitation and sexual abuse.

Most children who are sexually abused know their abusers. Most abusers are relatives or acquaintances of the child. A much smaller percentage of offenders are strangers. Most child sexual abuse is committed by men. Whatever the case, sexual abuse or exploitation is never the child's fault. The responsibility always lies with the abuser.

Every person has a unique reaction to sexual abuse or sexual exploitation, regardless of the type, extent or duration. Victims may show a range of emotional responses such as calm, anger, indifference or shock.

Some children may be exposed to life-threatening situations, such as sexually transmitted infections, including HIV. Girls may face the added risk of early and unwanted pregnancies that endanger their lives and can subject them to stigma and discrimination.

Children can begin to learn early on about 'good' touch versus 'bad' touch. Children can also be taught to tell an adult they trust if they have experienced a 'bad' touch. If a child comes to an adult with such information, the adult must take the child's claims seriously and immediately ensure that the abuse stops. The abuse should be reported to the authorities, and the child should receive protection services.

Many children and young people who have been victims of sexual abuse or exploitation heal and go on to lead normal lives. Sexual abuse in childhood does not automatically lead to sexually aggressive behaviour. Most sexual offenders have not been sexually abused as children, and most children who are sexually abused do not abuse others.

Governments are responsible for ensuring that systems and specific measures are in place to:

- prevent child abuse, violence and exploitation
- enable children to report abuse and exploitation
- make sure perpetrators of sexual abuse and exploitation are dealt with to the full extent of the law
- make social services, such as health care, psychosocial support, temporary care, education and legal assistance, timely and available for children who have been abused and exploited.

6.

Children are vulnerable to trafficking where protection for children is weak or missing. The government, civil society and families are responsible for preventing trafficking, as well as helping children who are victims to reintegrate into their families and communities, if it is in their best interest.

SUPPORTING INFORMATION

Trafficking of children is one of the fastest growing transnational crimes, occurring in and between countries. Profit from human trafficking has been estimated at approximately US$9.5 billion annually.

Children who are trafficked are:

- treated as commodities
- subject to violence, abuse, neglect, exploitation and HIV infection.

It is calculated that the majority of the children trafficked every year are girls who are sexually exploited.

Children and families burdened by poverty and with limited access to information may leave their communities because they believe better opportunities await them elsewhere. Sometimes children are promised a good education, a well-paying job or a better life. Instead they may find themselves smuggled or moved across borders or taken within their own country by traffickers and forced into dangerous situations. These may include domestic servitude, prostitution, forced marriage or begging.

It is important for children and families choosing to leave their communities to understand where they are going. They should know:

- what they can expect
- potential risks involved during travel as well as at the destination
- what to do if they get into a trafficking situation.

Governments can support local authorities and civil society to:

- distribute information to parents and children on the risks of migration and sending children away to work
- distribute information to communities on how negative attitudes towards migrant children can lead to social acceptance of child trafficking or indifference to it
- gain parental support to keep children in school and not allow them to drop out for work
- provide social services as needed to help reduce parents' dependence on their children's income or work
- address and reduce domestic violence, which can influence a child's decision to leave home
- treat children as victims of crime and not as criminals, and provide them with support and the time they need to recover before returning them to their families and communities or alternative care
- make and enforce laws that prosecute traffickers.

KEY MESSAGE

7.

Justice for children should be based on child rights. Depriving children of their liberty (incarcerating them) must always be a last resort. Procedures that are sensitive to children should be put in place for children who are victims or witnesses of crime.

SUPPORTING INFORMATION

Placing children who have committed crimes or have been accused of committing crimes in a detention centre, prison or reform school or any other closed setting should always be a last resort. Detention can be detrimental to children's development and make reintegration into society more difficult.

Alternatives such as mediation, community service and counselling produce better results for children and their families and communities. Such alternatives are generally more respectful of children's rights and help children learn how to take on a more constructive role in society. This should be the objective of all justice interventions concerning children.

The majority of children in detention have not committed a serious offence. They are often detained for dropping out of school, running away from home, using alcohol, begging or vagrancy. Some children are in detention because they have been exploited by adults through prostitution or drug dealing.

Children can remain in detention for months or years awaiting review of their case. These children are at higher risk of violence and exposure to drugs, HIV infection and other health problems. Detention can interrupt their schooling and distance them from family. Children in detention generally need a social protection response, not a judicial one.

Children who are in detention should:

- be separated from adult offenders
- have their cases addressed within a short time frame
- be separated by gender
- have appropriate means to report violence committed against them while in detention.

Pregnant women and mothers with children in detention need special protection, care and support. All children in these circumstances are entitled to protection of their rights, such as access to health care and education.

Child-sensitive procedures for boys and girls should be put in place for child victims and witnesses of crime. Such procedures should:

- prevent contact between the child and the alleged perpetrator (the person who is accused of committing the crime)
- allow for the child's full participation in the justice process
- ensure that the child is treated with dignity and compassion.

KEY MESSAGE

8.

Income support and social welfare services can help keep families together and children in school and ensure access to health care.

SUPPORTING INFORMATION

Households that need income support and social welfare services may be headed by the elderly, widows, children or individuals who are sick or disabled. This can include families affected by HIV.

Income support and social welfare services can provide children and families the means to:

- purchase food
- pay for or access health care and education
- keep families together
- keep children out of institutional care or from working or living on the street
- help families break out of the cycle of poverty.

The government and local authorities, with support from civil society, can help identify families in need. They can assist families with income support and social welfare services such as counselling and legal aid. It is important to ensure that families do not face discrimination related to accessing or using the services.

Information on income support and social welfare services can be provided through various communication channels, including health centres, schools and community centres; during community meetings and events; and through radio and loudspeaker announcements.

9.

All children have a right to age-appropriate information, to be heard and to participate in making decisions that concern them. Fulfilment of this right enables children to take an active role in their own protection against abuse, violence and exploitation, and to become active citizens.

SUPPORTING INFORMATION

From a very early age, including during infancy, girls and boys form and express views and interests. As they grow so does their ability to participate in decisions that concern them and their families and communities.

Children and adults should actively and consistently talk to each other, sharing information and ideas in the home, school and community. The exchange should be based on mutual respect. Children's views should be listened to and taken seriously in accordance with the child's age and maturity.

Girls and boys who express their opinions freely are more likely to assume responsibilities, develop critical thinking and communication skills, and make informed decisions as they grow. They are often able to:

- learn and perform better in school
- contribute to making responsible decisions regarding their education and health
- protect themselves against sexually transmitted infections, including HIV, unwanted pregnancy, bullying, bias, discrimination, harassment, violence, abuse and exploitation
- learn and practise active citizenship and grow into adults who will be ready to exercise their rights and responsibilities.

Children are avid users, producers and subjects of media, a powerful source for influencing opinion and perceptions among children. Different forms of media can be used responsibly to broaden children's knowledge, inform them on how to protect themselves and develop their citizenship skills.

Children-led associations or clubs can give girls and boys a place to voice their ideas, perspectives and concerns. Such clubs provide an opportunity for them to socialize and develop their interests and leadership skills.

Why it is important to share and act on information about
INJURY PREVENTION

Every year, nearly 1 million children die from injuries. Tens of millions more require hospital care for non-fatal injuries. Many are left with permanent disabilities or brain damage.

Injuries affect children of all ages. Girls and boys under 5 years of age are at particular risk. More boys than girls die from injuries.

The most common injuries are traffic injuries, non-fatal drowning (sometimes referred to as near drowning), burns, falls and poisoning.

Traffic injuries and drowning are the leading causes of injury-related death.

The most common place for young children to be injured is in or around their homes.

Almost all injuries can be prevented.

Families, communities and governments have an obligation to ensure children's right to live in a safe environment and be protected from injury.

1. Many serious injuries can be prevented if parents and other caregivers supervise children carefully and keep their environment safe.

2. Young children are at risk on or near roads. They should not play on or near the road and should always have someone older with them when they are near or crossing a road. They should wear a helmet when on a bicycle or motorcycle and should be securely strapped into an age-appropriate child restraint when being transported in a vehicle.

3. Children can drown in less than two minutes and in a very small amount of water, even in a bathtub. They should never be left alone in or near water.

4. Burns can be prevented by keeping children away from fires, cooking stoves, hot liquids and foods, and exposed electric wires.

5. Falls are a major cause of injury for young children. Stairs, balconies, roofs, windows, and play and sleeping areas should be made secure, using barriers with vertical bars to protect children from falling.

6. Medicines, poisons, insecticides, bleach, acids and liquid fertilizers and fuels, such as paraffin (kerosene), should be stored carefully out of children's sight and reach. Dangerous substances should be stored in clearly marked containers and never in drinking bottles. Child-resistant closures, where available, should be used on the containers of poisonous products.

7. Knives, scissors, sharp or pointed objects and broken glass can cause serious injuries. These objects should be kept out of children's reach. Plastic bags, which can cause suffocation, should be kept away from young children.

8. Young children like to put things in their mouths. To prevent choking, small objects, such as coins, nuts and buttons, should be kept out of their reach. Children's foods should be cut into small pieces that can be easily chewed and swallowed.

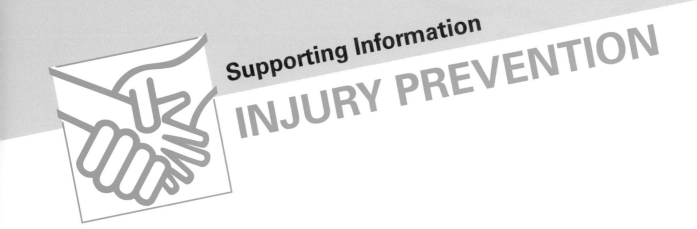

KEY MESSAGE

1.

Many serious injuries can be prevented if parents and other caregivers supervise children carefully and keep their environment safe.

SUPPORTING INFORMATION

Young children, especially as they begin to move around on their own – and particularly between 12 months and 4 years old – are at high risk of injuries in and near the home. Almost all these injuries can be prevented. Prevention requires supervising children carefully and keeping them away from dangers, such as cooking fires, water sources, places where they can fall, roads, and items that can poison, choke or hurt them.

2.

Young children are at risk on or near the roads. They should not play on or near the road and should always have someone older with them when they are near or crossing a road. They should wear a helmet when on a bicycle or motorcycle and should be securely strapped into an age-appropriate child restraint when being transported in a vehicle.

SUPPORTING INFORMATION

Children may be hurt when they are crossing or walking along roads, or if they play near roads. Young children do not think before they run onto the road.

Families need to:

- watch children carefully
- fence the house and close the gate to prevent young children from running onto the road
- teach young children never to cross or walk along a road unless accompanied by an adult or older child
- prevent children from playing near the road
- teach children not to run after balls, moving toys or kites that go on or near the road
- instruct children to walk on the side of the road, facing traffic
- if there is a sidewalk, teach children to use it rather than walk on the road.

When crossing the road, young children should be taught to:

- stop at the side of the road
- look both ways
- listen for cars or other vehicles before crossing
- hold the hand of another person
- walk, not run
- in urban areas, use pedestrian crossings
- avoid crossing the road at a curve or between parked cars
- avoid crossing roads with high-speed traffic.

Children are also at high risk of serious injury if they travel in the front seat of a car, unsupervised on the bed of a truck or agricultural machinery, or on a motorcycle.

In a car, children should use an age-appropriate child restraint or a booster seat until they are 150 centimetres tall or 10 years old, when they are big enough to use an adult seat belt.

While travelling with parents or other caregivers on a motorbike, all passengers, including children, should wear a helmet that is securely strapped under the chin so it cannot come off in case of an accident.

Bicycle accidents are a frequent cause of injury and death among children. All children should learn road safety and wear a bicycle helmet when riding a bike.

For first aid advice on injuries, refer to the end of this chapter.

KEY MESSAGE

3.

Children can drown in less than two minutes and in a very small amount of water, even in a bathtub. They should never be left alone in or near water.

SUPPORTING INFORMATION

Drowning may cause brain injury or death. To prevent children from drowning, parents and other caregivers should always closely supervise children who are near or in the water.

Where there is water, it is important to:

- cover wells and water tanks so children cannot open them
- turn tubs and buckets upside down when not in use, and always supervise children taking a bath
- teach children to stay away from ditches and drains
- for families who live near bodies of water, install a fence around the house and close the gates to prevent young children from going in the water
- fence ponds and pools with vertical rails spaced close together to prevent children from getting through them to the water
- for families who live directly on the water, put vertical bars on terraces, windows and doors to prevent young children from falling in the water
- teach children how to swim when they are young
- have young children and children who cannot swim wear an approved flotation device (life jacket) when playing in the water or on a boat
- always supervise children who are swimming
- teach children never to swim in fast-flowing streams and never to swim alone
- in flood-prone areas, carefully watch children when the water begins to rise; make sure that all family members, including children old enough to understand, are well informed of safe places to go to if they need to leave the home quickly.

For first aid advice on drowning, refer to the end of this chapter.

4.

SUPPORTING INFORMATION

Burning and scalding are among the most common causes of serious injury among young children. Burns often cause permanent scarring, and some are fatal. The great majority of these are preventable.

One of the most common types of burns is from direct contact with fires or flames or touching hot surfaces. To prevent this kind of burn:

- keep young children away from cooking fires, matches, paraffin lamps, candles and flammable liquids such as paraffin and kerosene

- put stoves on a flat, raised surface out of the reach of children

- if an open cooking fire is used, make it on a raised mound of clay, not directly on the ground. A barrier of mud, bamboo or other material or a playpen can also be used to keep young children out of reach of the cooking place.

- do not leave small children alone near fires or to tend fires or cook

- keep children away from heaters, hot irons and other hot appliances

- never leave a child alone in a room with a candle or fire burning.

Another major cause of burns is scalding from hot liquids or foods. To prevent scalds:

- turn the handles of all cooking pots away from the reach of children

- keep hot foods and liquids in a safe place and out of children's reach

- do not let children turn on the hot water tap in a bath or shower by themselves

- keep the temperature of water heaters below a medium setting to prevent scalding if children turn on the hot water

- teach children not to play rough around people with hot drinks or in the kitchen when meals are being prepared

- never hold a child when having hot liquids or foods.

Children can get a serious shock or burn if they come in contact with electricity. To prevent shocks and burns:

- teach children never to put their fingers or other objects into electric sockets

- cover power sockets to prevent access

INJURY PREVENTION

- keep electric wires out of children's reach

- cover bare electric wires, which are particularly dangerous, using insulating tape.

For first aid advice on burns, refer to the end of this chapter.

5.

Falls are a major cause of injury for young children. Stairs, balconies, roofs, windows, and play and sleeping areas should be made secure, using barriers with vertical bars to protect children from falling.

SUPPORTING INFORMATION

Children often fall as they learn to walk, run and jump. Many of these falls cause small scrapes and bruises. Sometimes falls can cause broken bones, head injuries or other serious injuries, even death.

Infants left unattended may fall from beds, cots or hammocks. Young children may fall down stairs or from windows or balconies.

Children like to climb. They can be seriously injured if they fall from a high place or try to climb up on top of heavy furniture that might fall on them.

In addition to supervision, some steps to prevent children from serious falls include:

- discourage and prevent children from climbing onto unsafe places

- do not allow children to play on stairs and balconies, and, if they do, watch them closely

- use railings of appropriate width and height with vertical bars on stairs, windows or balconies

- keep the home clean, well lit and free of sharp objects and rough edges

- properly secure babies in high chairs

- do not leave infants unattended on beds, cots, hammocks or in walkers or other baby equipment

- keep furniture such as beds, chairs and cribs away from windows

- do not put toys or other items on high shelves that may attract small children, and fasten heavy furniture such as cabinets or shelves to the wall.

For first aid advice on broken bones, bruises or sprains, refer to the end of this chapter.

6.

Medicines, poisons, insecticides, bleach, acids and liquid fertilizers and fuels, such as paraffin (kerosene), should be stored carefully out of children's sight and reach. Dangerous substances should be stored in clearly marked containers and never in drinking bottles. Child-resistant closures, where available, should be used on the containers of poisonous products.

SUPPORTING INFORMATION

Poisoning is a serious danger to small children. Bleach, insect and rat poison, paraffin (kerosene) and household detergents can kill or permanently injure a child.

Many poisons can kill, cause brain damage, blind or permanently injure if they:

- are swallowed
- are inhaled
- get onto the skin
- get into the eyes.

The key to preventing poisoning is to keep harmful substances out of children's reach.

- Poisons should never be put in soft drink or beer bottles, jars or cups, as children may drink them by mistake. All medicines, chemicals and poisons should be stored in their original containers, tightly sealed and out of children's reach.

- Detergents, bleaches, chemicals and medicines should never be left where children can reach them. They should be tightly sealed and labelled. They should also be locked in a cupboard or trunk or put on a high shelf where children cannot see or reach them.

- Medicines meant for adults can kill or injure small children. Medicine should only be given to a child if it is prescribed for that child. It should never be given to a child if it is prescribed for an adult or some other child. A child should never take medication on his or her own. The parent or other caregiver should give the medication to the child each time it is needed. Medication should be stored out of reach and sight of children.

- Child-resistant closures, where available, should be used on containers storing poisonous substances.

For first aid advice on poisoning, refer to the end of this chapter.

7.

Knives, scissors, sharp or pointed objects and broken glass can cause serious injuries. These objects should be kept out of children's reach. Plastic bags, which can cause suffocation, should be kept away from young children.

Broken glass can cause serious cuts, loss of blood and infected wounds. Sharp metal objects, machinery and rusty cans can cause wounds that can become badly infected.

Families can reduce the risk of children's injuries from glass and sharp objects if they:

- keep glass bottles out of reach of young children and keep the house and play area free of broken glass and refuse

- place knives, razors and scissors in drawers or locked cabinets well out of reach of young children

- safely dispose of household refuse, including broken bottles and old cans.

Other injuries around the home can be prevented by teaching children about the dangers of throwing stones or other sharp objects and of playing with knives or scissors.

Plastic bags should be kept away from young children to prevent suffocation.

For first aid advice on cuts and wounds, refer to the end of this chapter.

8.

Young children like to put things in their mouths. To prevent choking, small objects, such as coins, nuts and buttons, should be kept out of their reach. Children's foods should be cut into small pieces that can be easily chewed and swallowed.

SUPPORTING INFORMATION

One way young children explore their environment is by putting things in their mouths which might cause them to choke. Also, young children have difficulty chewing and swallowing some foods such as hard sweets that can cause them to choke.

Parents or other caregivers should:

- keep play and sleeping areas free of small objects such as buttons, beads, balloons, pen caps, coins, seeds and nuts

- check new toys carefully before children play with them to make sure they have no loose or sharp pieces that could break and be swallowed by or hurt the child

- never give young children foods they can choke on such as groundnuts (peanuts), hard sweets or food with small bones or seeds

- always supervise young children during meals, and cut or tear children's food into small pieces that can be easily chewed or swallowed.

Coughing, gagging and high-pitched, noisy breathing or the inability to make any sound at all indicate breathing difficulty and possible choking. Parents and other caregivers should suspect a child is choking when he or she suddenly has trouble breathing, even if no one has seen the child put something into the mouth.

For first aid advice on choking, refer to the end of this chapter.

INJURY PREVENTION

FIRST AID ADVICE

Until medical help is available, the following first aid measures should help prevent a situation from becoming worse. Parents, other caregivers and older children should be supported in learning about these first aid measures.

First aid for burns:	• If the child's clothing catches fire, quickly wrap the child in a blanket or clothing or roll him or her on the ground to put out the fire.
For minor burns, the following steps can be taken:	• Cool the burned area immediately. Use plenty of cold, clean water, which helps to reduce pain and swelling. Do not put ice on the burn; this can further damage the skin.
	• Keep the burn clean and dry with a loose sterile gauze bandage or clean cloth. This will protect blistered skin.
	• Do not break blisters, as they protect the injured area. If a blister is broken, the area is more susceptible to infection. Do not apply butter or ointments to the burn; they can prevent proper healing.
	• A minor burn will usually heal without further treatment.
For major burns that burn all layers of skin, emergency care is needed immediately. Until it is available, the following steps can be taken:	• Do not remove the burned clothing from the body. Make sure the child is no longer near any burning or smouldering materials or exposed to smoke or heat.
	• Do not immerse large, serious burns in cold water, as this could cause shock.
	• Raise the burned body part or parts above heart level, if possible.
	• Loosely cover the burn area with cool, moist towels or cloths or a sterile bandage.
	• If the child is unconscious, keep him or her warm. Roll the child onto his or her side so that the tongue does not block breathing.
	• Check for signs of breathing, movement and coughing. If there are no signs, follow the steps under 'First aid for breathing problems or drowning'.

First aid for broken bones, bruises or sprains:	• A child who is unable to move or is in extreme pain may have broken bones. Do not move the injured area and get medical help immediately.
	• For bad bruises and sprains, immerse the injured area in cold water or put ice on the injury for 15 minutes. Do not put the ice directly on the skin; use a layer of cloth between the ice and the skin. Remove the ice or water, wait 15 minutes and repeat, if necessary. The cold should help reduce pain, swelling and bruising.

First aid for cuts and wounds:

For minor cuts and wounds:

• Wash the wound with clean (or boiled and cooled) water and soap.

• Dry the skin around the wound.

• Cover the wound with a clean cloth and place a sterile bandage over it.

For serious cuts and wounds:

• If a piece of glass or other object is sticking in the wound, do not remove it. It may be preventing further bleeding, and removing it could make the injury worse.

• If the child is bleeding heavily, raise the injured area above the level of the chest and press firmly against the wound (or near it if something is stuck in it) with a pad made of folded clean cloth. Maintain pressure until the bleeding stops.

• Do not put any plant or animal matter on the wound, as this could cause infection.

• Put a clean sterile bandage on the wound. Allow for swelling by not tying the bandage too tightly.

• Seek medical help immediately. Ask a trained health worker if the child should have a tetanus injection.

INJURY PREVENTION

First aid for choking:

- If an infant or child is coughing, let him or her try to cough up the object. If the object does not release quickly, try to remove the object from the child's mouth.

- If the object is still lodged in the child's throat:

For infants or young children:

- Support the head and neck.

- Turn the baby or young child face down with the head lower than the feet. Deliver five careful blows to the back between the shoulder blades. Turn the baby face up and press firmly on the breastbone between the nipples five times. Repeat (face down and face up) until the object is dislodged.

- If you cannot dislodge the object, take the child to the nearest health worker immediately.

For larger children:

- Stand behind the child with your arms around the child's waist.

- Form a clenched fist with your thumb against the child's body, above the navel and below the rib cage.

- Put the other hand over the fist and give a sharp inward and upward thrust into the child's abdomen. Repeat until the object is dislodged.

- If you cannot dislodge the object, take the child to the nearest health worker immediately.

First aid for breathing problems or drowning:

- If there is any possibility of injury to the head or neck, do not move the child's head. Follow the breathing directions below without moving the head.

- If the child is having difficulty breathing or is not breathing, lay the child flat on the back and tilt her or his head back slightly. Pinch the child's nostrils closed and blow (breathe) into the mouth, keeping all the mouth covered. Blow gently but hard enough to make the child's chest rise. Then, count to three and blow again. Continue until the child begins breathing.

- If the child is breathing but unconscious, roll the child onto his or her side so the tongue does not block breathing.

- If a person who cannot swim sees a child drowning in deep water, the person should immediately throw a rope, floating device or tree branch to the child and shout loudly so that others can come to help rescue the child.

First aid for poisoning:

- If a child has swallowed poison, do not try to make the child vomit. This may make the child more ill.

- If poison is on the child's skin or clothes, remove the clothing and pour large amounts of water over the skin. Wash the skin thoroughly several times with soap.

- If a child gets poison in his or her eyes, splash clean water in the eyes for at least 10 minutes.

- Take the child immediately to a health centre or hospital if any of these situations occur. If possible, bring a sample of the poison or medicine or its container with you. Keep the child as still and quiet as possible.

- If a child is bitten by a venomous or rabid animal, it is important to see a health-care provider immediately for treatment.

Why it is important to share and act on information about

EMERGENCIES: PREPAREDNESS AND RESPONSE

Emergencies, such as conflicts, disasters or epidemics, expose families to risks that make them especially vulnerable to disease, malnutrition and violence. With the right information and support, families and communities can establish measures that map out what to do in an emergency.

Girls, boys and women typically are the most affected by emergencies. An estimated 26 million people were displaced by armed conflicts and violence in 2007. Each year, up to 50 million people are displaced due to disasters. Climate change could increase these numbers.

Displacement undermines families' livelihoods and social support mechanisms. This can lead to family separations and increase children's vulnerability to discrimination, abuse, violence, poverty and exploitation.

Conflict and disasters put children at risk of disease and malnutrition. Access to health services is reduced, and food shortages are common. Water can become scarce, especially when access is limited by overcrowding and poor sanitary conditions. Children's access to education is often undermined, since schools are frequently targeted for attacks and abductions, and teachers and materials are in short supply. The risk of HIV transmission increases in such contexts.

In situations of conflict, girls and boys are particularly vulnerable to forced recruitment by armed forces and groups. Along with women, they are also at risk of abduction, trafficking and sexual violence, including rape.

Epidemics (or outbreaks) of diseases can be caused by emergencies or can by themselves cause an emergency. The emergency can arise because of the severe nature of the disease or the community's response to it.

A pandemic is a widespread, usually global, epidemic. An influenza pandemic results from a new influenza virus against which the population has little or no immunity. It can spread rapidly across the world and is recurrent and unpredictable. The youngest children, under 2 years of age, are particularly vulnerable to influenza and other infectious diseases.

Children and their family members have the right to protection and the information and support they may need to prepare for and cope with such complex situations.

KEY MESSAGES:
What every family and community
has a right to know about

EMERGENCIES: PREPAREDNESS AND RESPONSE

1. In emergencies, children have the same rights as in non-emergency situations. This is true whether the emergency is a conflict, disaster or epidemic.

2. Girls and boys and their families and communities should plan ahead and take simple steps to prepare for emergencies – at home, at school and in the community.

3. Measles, diarrhoea, pneumonia, malaria, malnutrition and neonatal complications are major causes of child deaths, particularly during emergencies.

4. An epidemic (or outbreak) of disease can cause an emergency because of the severity of the disease or responses to it. In the case of pandemic influenza and other diseases spread by close personal contact, those who are ill should be kept separated from others.

5. Mothers, even malnourished mothers, can still breastfeed even under the stressful conditions of emergencies.

6. Children have the right to be protected from violence in emergencies. Governments, civil society, international organizations, communities and families have the responsibility to protect them.

7. It is generally preferable for children to be cared for by their parents or other usual caregivers because it makes children feel more secure. If separation occurs, every effort should be made to reunite the child with his or her family, if it is in the child's best interest.

8. The disruption and stress caused by disasters and armed conflict can frighten and anger children. When such events occur, children need special attention and extra affection. They should be kept as safe as possible and supported in resuming normal activities. Children can be given age-appropriate opportunities to participate in the responses to and decisions regarding the emergency situation.

9. Children have the right to education, even during emergencies. Having children attend a safe, child-friendly school helps to reinforce their sense of normalcy and start the process of healing.

10. Landmines and unexploded devices are extremely dangerous. They can explode and kill or disable many people if touched, stepped on or disturbed in any way. Children and their families should stay only in areas that have been declared safe and avoid unknown objects.

EMERGENCIES: PREPAREDNESS AND RESPONSE

KEY MESSAGE

1.

In emergencies, children have the same rights as in non-emergency situations. This is true whether the emergency is a conflict, disaster or epidemic.

SUPPORTING INFORMATION

All children and their families and communities have the right to receive humanitarian assistance in emergencies.

Children and their families who are forced from their homes by conflicts or disasters have the same rights as those living in their homes and communities in non-emergency situations.

Communities can designate protected areas to shelter civilians and the sick. These areas must never be used for any military purposes.

Humanitarian relief workers and supplies must always be respected and protected. Combatants should always allow all civilians access to humanitarian assistance.

The particular needs of women and adolescent girls in emergency situations must be respected. Their specific needs of privacy, hygiene and protection must be taken into account. Unaccompanied children, pregnant women, mothers with young children, female heads-of-households, persons with disabilities and the elderly may require specific attention to address their particular needs.

When children and families are displaced within a country, the national authorities have the primary responsibility to protect children's rights and assist children and families. The United Nations, non-governmental organizations and the International Committee of the Red Cross (ICRC), among others, also have a critical role to play in providing assistance and protection to children and families.

Displaced persons have the right to safely return to their homes as soon as the reasons for their displacement are no longer an issue. The property rights of displaced persons must be respected so children and families can rebuild their lives.

As communities begin to re-establish and reconstruct after an emergency, attention should be given to providing social services, including health and education, to children, women and families.

Humanitarian workers who provide aid to civilians should minimize opportunities for violence, exploitation and abuse. Any activity by humanitarian workers that exploits the population should be reported immediately to the agency concerned and the authorities.

2.

Girls and boys and their families and communities should plan ahead and take simple steps to prepare for emergencies – at home, at school and in the community.

SUPPORTING INFORMATION

Within the household, the whole family can prepare for an emergency brought about by a disaster or conflict. Everyone should be aware of the different dangers of fire, earthquakes, floods, storms and other hazards and the risks during conflicts. The response can be more effective when everyone in the family and community knows how to reduce their risks and understands their responsibilities.

The possible dangers and safe areas in and around a community should be identified. If possible they should be shown on a local map. Everybody in the community should be involved and informed. Plans should include how young children, older people and people who are unwell would be assisted.

Community warning systems and evacuation routes for escaping from danger should be well identified and communicated. Communities can hold simulated drills of safety measures with boys and girls in schools and with families in neighbourhoods.

Communities should ensure that health facilities are well built to withstand emergencies and function in their wake. Health-care staff must be trained so they are prepared to act in emergency situations.

It is important for schools to be located in a safe place, close to where children live and away from disaster-prone areas, such as where flooding or mudslides might occur. Schools should be well constructed to ensure the safety of children and teachers. They should be carefully organized to protect children from attacks, abduction or other forms of violence.

Teachers and school administrators can help children, their families and communities to:

- understand natural hazards and other emergency risks

- know how to prevent disaster

- know what to do in an emergency.

Families, including children, should be encouraged to recognize a warning and understand what to do when they see or hear it. A warning or signal can be as simple as a whistle, horn or coloured flag. Safe locations where families can meet should be identified. Safe places for domestic animals should also be identified. These precautions help to prevent family separation.

Children can be trained to memorize their name and the names of their relatives and their village or town. They can be trained to identify geographical indicators or landmarks that might locate their community if they get separated from their families.

A family emergency bag prepared in advance can be life-saving. It should include a torch (flashlight), batteries, candles, matches, radio, water container and first aid kit. The packet should be checked periodically and ready at all times.

Birth certificates and other important family documents should be kept in a safe, easily accessible place. Storing them in plastic wrap helps protect them from water and damage.

3.

Measles, diarrhoea, pneumonia, malaria, malnutrition and neonatal complications are major causes of child deaths, particularly during emergencies.

Infectious diseases spread easily in crowded emergency conditions. To reduce the risks:

- ensure that all children 6 months to 15 years of age are appropriately immunized, especially against measles, at the first point of contact or settlement

- continue to seek health-care services to prevent and treat illnesses.

(*Refer to the chapters on Safe Motherhood and Newborn Health, Immunizations, Coughs, Colds and More Serious Illnesses, and Malaria.*)

Malnutrition is more common in emergencies due to shortages of food, increased disease and disruption of caring practices. It is therefore important to ensure that children:

- breastfeed and receive adequate amounts of age-appropriate nutritious foods and drinks

- receive micronutrient supplements in addition to fortified foods.

Children who are very thin and/or swollen (usually the feet and legs) need to be taken to a trained health worker or health facility for immediate assessment and treatment and further management in accordance with their status.

(*Refer to the chapters on Breastfeeding, and Nutrition and Growth.*)

In emergencies, lack of safe water, sanitation and hygiene can cause disease that may turn into an epidemic. Cholera can occur where there is poor sanitation and overcrowding. Basic steps to follow include:

- continue to wash hands frequently with soap and water or a substitute, such as ash and water

- dispose of faeces and garbage safely

- practise safe food preparation

- use safe water sources or employ home-based water treatment, such as boiling, filtering, adding chlorine or disinfecting with sunlight

- store safe water in clean, covered containers.

(*Refer to the chapters on Hygiene and Diarrhoea.*)

4.

An epidemic (or outbreak) of disease can cause an emergency because of the severity of the disease or responses to it. In the case of pandemic influenza and other diseases spread by close personal contact, those who are ill should be kept separated from others.

SUPPORTING INFORMATION

The impact of a disease outbreak depends on the severity of the disease as well as the responses by governments, communities and individuals.

An influenza pandemic, involving a new virus, can spread rapidly through a population that has little or no immunity against the new virus. The influenza might be moderate or severe in terms of the illness and death it causes. The outbreak can come and go repeatedly over time. Its level of severity can change over the course of the pandemic, making it unpredictable. It generally has a greater impact than regular seasonal influenza outbreaks.

Annual or seasonal influenza causes most deaths in people over 65 years of age. An influenza pandemic causes more severe illness and deaths in younger age groups. In both seasonal and pandemic influenza, pregnant women and children under 2 years old are at increased risk of complications and death. Older children have the highest rates of infection but tend not to have severe outcomes.

Influenza symptoms include high fever, cough, sore throat, body aches, headache, chills, fatigue, vomiting and diarrhoea. In some cases, influenza can lead to pneumonia and breathing difficulties.

During an outbreak of influenza or other infection, some general steps to help protect children and families include:

- stay home if sick, and stay apart from others
- know the symptoms and danger signs, and what to do and where to go to get help if the illness becomes severe
- wash hands with soap and water often, and keep surfaces clean
- cough or sneeze into an elbow or a tissue, and dispose safely of tissues
- do not spit near children or in public.

In an outbreak of an infection that has serious consequences, it is important to reduce close contact with others:

- stay at least one metre apart from others, especially if they are coughing or sneezing or look unwell
- stay at home as much as possible and avoid public gatherings and travel.

In an extensive outbreak, some individuals may need to be isolated in a hospital setting for treatment or to prevent the spread of the infection. But for many people access to care may be limited.

To care for sick people at home and to prevent the spread of the infection in the household:

- give sick people a separate space at home
- assign a single caregiver to a sick person
- give plenty of fluids and foods to the sick person.

5.

Mothers, even malnourished mothers, can still breastfeed even under the stressful conditions of emergencies.

SUPPORTING INFORMATION

People often believe that during emergencies many mothers can no longer breastfeed due to stress or inadequate nutrition. This is a misconception – *it is not correct*. Mothers who lack food or who are undernourished can still breastfeed adequately. They should be given extra fluids and foods to protect their health and well-being and that of the child. Fathers and other family members can support breastfeeding mothers with food preparation and childcare.

Stress can temporarily interfere with the flow of breastmilk. But it does not need to stop breastmilk production, if mothers and infants remain together and are supported in initiating and continuing breastfeeding. Safe havens, as in refugee camps and shelters, can be established where women can go to receive support.

In some cases breastfeeding is not possible. These include children temporarily or permanently separated from their mothers, mothers who are very sick, mothers who have stopped breastfeeding for some time, mothers who have not been able to restart breastfeeding, and HIV-positive mothers who have chosen not to breastfeed.

In these situations, for children under 12 months, the most appropriate food is a high-quality breastmilk substitute (infant formula). Safe preparaton of the breastmilk substitute requires fuel, safe water and equipment, and preferably the guidance of a trained health worker. The breastmilk substitute should be stored and prepared under hygienic conditions with water from a safe source, using a cup, not a bottle.

Breastmilk substitutes should never be distributed in an uncontrolled manner alongside food aid and without attention to the conditions required for safe preparation. They should not displace breastfeeding, a baby's best protection against illness in an emergency situation.

KEY MESSAGE

6.

Children have the right to be protected from violence in emergencies. Governments, civil society, international organizations, communities and families have the responsibility to protect them.

SUPPORTING INFORMATION

Protecting girls and boys during conflicts or disasters is critical since they can be vulnerable to many kinds of violence.

Some violence is directly related to the emergency. This includes abduction, torture, beating, harassment and injuries during fighting by soldiers or armed groups or fighting in communities over limited resources. Emergencies also increase the usual risks of violence in a community, such as domestic violence, violence in schools or violence among children themselves.

Girls and women are at particular risk of trafficking and sexual violence, including rape, which is sometimes used as a tactic of war. *This is unacceptable.* All efforts should be taken by governments and local authorities to make sure this *never* happens. Girls and women who are subjected to this violence need health care, psychosocial support and counselling. Some will need support in relocating and reintegrating into their families.

In armed conflicts, children must be protected. They must not be recruited by armed forces or armed groups or be allowed to take part in fighting. If children are arrested, they should not be harmed. They should be kept separate from adults (or with their family), and they must receive a fair trial. If girls or boys are victims of violence, they have the right to seek justice that takes their views into account.

It is important for children and families to report violations against children's rights to the authorities when it is safe to do so. Serious violations of children's rights, including killing children, using children as soldiers, sexual violence against children and abduction of children, should be reported to international humanitarian agencies.

7.

It is generally preferable for children to be cared for by their parents or other usual caregivers because it makes children feel more secure. If separation occurs, every effort should be made to reunite the child with his or her family, if it is in the child's best interest.

SUPPORTING INFORMATION

In emergencies, it is the duty of the government or the authorities in charge to ensure that children are not separated from their parents or other caregivers.

If separation occurs, the government or authorities in charge have the responsibility to provide special protection and care for these children. They should first register all unaccompanied, separated and orphaned children and make sure their essential needs are met.

Every effort should then be made to find the child's family and to reunite the child with his or her family, if it is in the best interest of the child.

Interim care must be provided for children separated from their families. Where possible this can be provided by the child's extended family or by a family from the child's community until the child is reunited with parents or relatives or placed with a foster family. Every effort should be made to keep siblings together.

If a child is temporarily placed in a foster family, it is the duty of those responsible for the placement to follow up on the child's care and well-being. They should also ensure that the foster family is provided with the means to adequately care for the child.

Children who have become separated from their parents in an emergency cannot be assumed to be orphans. They are not available for adoption. As long as the fate of a child's parents and/or other close relatives cannot be determined, each separated child must be assumed to have parents and/or close relatives who are still living.

Long-term care arrangements should not be made during an emergency. After a suitable period of investigation, if parents or relatives cannot be traced or are not available to care for the child, a foster family or domestic adoptive family, preferably in the child's community, should be found for the child. Childcare institutions or orphanages should always be considered a temporary measure and a last resort.

A move to a new community or country can be stressful, especially if the child's family has fled violence or a disaster. Displaced children sometimes may have to learn a new language and culture. Often, schools and community organizations can assist children and their families with the transition and integration into their new community.

8.

The disruption and stress caused by disasters and armed conflict can frighten and anger children. When such events occur, children need special attention and extra affection. They should be kept as safe as possible and supported in resuming normal activities. Children can be given age-appropriate opportunities to participate in the responses to and decisions regarding the emergency situation.

SUPPORTING INFORMATION

It is normal for children's feelings and behaviours to be affected by frightening, painful or violent experiences. Children react differently – they may lose interest in daily life, become more aggressive or turn very fearful. Some children who appear to be coping well are hiding their emotions and fears.

Parents or regular caregivers, peers, teachers and community members are an important source of support and security for children. Families and communities can help children if they:

- listen to both girls and boys and provide them opportunities to express their concerns, participate in decision-making and find solutions

- provide children with age-appropriate information, reassurance and emotional support

- maintain familiar routines in daily life and resume normal activities as soon as possible

- provide enjoyable age-appropriate activities for children such as cultural activities, visits to friends and families, and sports

- encourage children to continue to play and socialize with others

- provide children with age-appropriate opportunities to participate in meaningful ways in everyday activities and in the emergency response, such as assisting with teaching and caring for young children

- maintain clear rules for acceptable behaviour and avoid physical punishment

- provide safe spaces where children and parents can socialize, learn life skills and access basic services

- help children learn how to manage their stress.

When children's stress reactions are severe and last for a long time, they need help from a qualified professional such as a counsellor, psychologist or specialized nurse or doctor.

9.

Children have the right to education, even during emergencies. Having children attend a safe, child-friendly school helps to reinforce their sense of normalcy and start the process of healing.

Regular routines, such as going to school and maintaining normal eating and sleeping schedules, give children a sense of security and continuity.

Child-friendly schools and spaces can provide a protective and safe learning environment for all children coping with an emergency.

With support from families and communities, teachers and school administrators can help:

- provide a safe, structured place for children to learn and play
- identify children who are experiencing stress, trauma or family separation and provide basic psychosocial support
- provide a daily routine and a sense of the future beyond the emergency
- ensure that children retain and develop basic literacy and numeracy skills
- provide children with life-saving health and security information and skills to reduce their risks
- provide a place for expression through play, sports, music, drama and art
- facilitate integration of vulnerable children into the school and community
- support networking and interaction with and among families
- provide children with an understanding of human rights and skills for living in peace
- build awareness with children on how to protect the environment and develop their skills to reduce disaster risks
- encourage children to analyse information, express opinions and take action on particular issues important to them.

Teachers require support and training to understand and deal with children's and their own stressful experiences, losses and reactions to emergencies. They need to know how to give emotional, mental and spiritual support to students and guide families on how to do the same with their children.

Schools and communities can also help to organize fun activities for children outside of school time. Opportunities can be created for organized non-violent play, sports and other forms of recreation. Communication and interaction among peers should be encouraged and supported. Use of arts such as drawing, or playing with toys or puppets, can help young children express their concerns and adjust to stressful experiences.

Parents and other caregivers should keep children who become sick with the flu or other infectious disease at home or in their place of residence if displaced from their homes.

In case of a severe epidemic that spreads rapidly from person to person, local authorities and education personnel need to make appropriate decisions regarding how to protect children. As a public health measure, classes may be suspended to reduce spread of the disease. In such cases, education can still continue by using alternative strategies. This requires good planning and follow-up by education personnel in collaboration with the students' families.

KEY MESSAGE

10.

Landmines and unexploded devices are extremely dangerous. They can explode and kill or disable many people if touched, stepped on or disturbed in any way. Children and their families should stay only in areas that have been declared safe and avoid unknown objects.

SUPPORTING INFORMATION

Landmines are victim-activated explosive devices intended to kill or injure people or destroy or damage vehicles. Unexploded ordnance (called UXO) are any munitions, such as bombs, shells, mortars or grenades, that were used but failed to detonate as intended.

Both landmines and UXO come in many different shapes, sizes and colours. They can be buried underground, placed above ground or hidden in grass, trees or water. They may be bright and shiny or dirty and rusty, but they are always dangerous and must be avoided at all times.

Landmines are usually not visible. Special caution is needed near areas of military action or abandoned or overgrown areas. Dangerous areas are often designated by a marking such as a picture of a skull and crossbones, red-painted stones or other common markings that draw attention and are easily recognized as hazard warnings by the local population.

UXO are often easier to see than landmines. Their colour and shape make them attractive to children, but they are extremely dangerous and unstable. They can explode with the slightest touch or change in temperature. They kill more often than do landmines.

Children should be taught not to touch unfamiliar objects. They need to learn that if anything looks suspicious they should keep away and inform adults they know or the authorities.

Since some roads may be mined or littered with explosive remnants of war, it is important for families to ask local people which roads or paths are safe to travel. Generally it is safer to travel on commonly used roads and paths.

Places likely to have mines, UXO or abandoned weapons and ammunition include abandoned or destroyed buildings, unused paths or roads, untouched and overgrown fields, current or former military bases, outposts, checkpoints, trenches or ditches. Children and their families need to be informed to stay away from these areas. Measures should be put in place to keep them away.

Children and their families need to learn what to do if they see a mine or UXO. They should:

- stand still and tell others nearby to do the same
- avoid panicking
- avoid movement
- call for help
- if help does not come, carefully consider the options before moving to retrace the original steps backwards very slowly.

If a landmine or UXO injury occurs:

- apply firm pressure to the bleeding area until the bleeding stops
- if the bleeding is not stopping, tie a cloth or piece of clothing (a tourniquet) just above or as close to the wound as possible and send for medical assistance
- if help is delayed more than one hour, loosen the tourniquet hourly to check the bleeding; remove the tourniquet when the bleeding stops
- if the person is breathing but unconscious, roll the person onto his or her side so the tongue does not block breathing
- seek follow-up medical care, as needed.

Governments and local authorities have the responsibility to make communities safe for all children and families. Professional demining is the best solution to ensure the safety of all.

Facts for Life
GLOSSARY

ACTs	artemisinin-based combination therapies that treat *Plasmodium falciparum* malaria, the most serious type of malaria, which causes nearly all malaria deaths
AIDS	acquired immunodeficiency syndrome
ART	antiretroviral therapy – a group of medicines used to treat HIV
anaemia	a blood deficiency that results in poor health, commonly caused by lack of iron in the diet
BCG	Bacille Calmette-Guérin – an anti-tuberculosis vaccine
DTP or DPT	diphtheria and tetanus toxoid with pertussis (whooping cough) vaccine
eclampsia	an illness that sometimes occurs during the later stages of pregnancy, which involves high blood pressure and can cause convulsions, sometimes followed by a coma
expressed milk	milk removed from the breast manually or by using a pump
FGM/C	female genital mutilation/cutting is any procedure that involves partial or total removal of the external female genitalia or other injury to the female genital organs for non-medical reasons
fistula (obstetric)	an abnormal opening between a woman's vagina and her bladder and/or rectum, through which urine and/or faeces continually leak; obstetric fistula is caused by complications during childbirth
goitre	an enlargement of the thyroid gland that causes a swelling of the neck and is a sign of iodine deficiency in the person's diet
HepB	Hepatitis B vaccine
Hib	*Haemophilus influenzae* type B vaccine
HIV	human immunodeficiency virus
infibulation	the most extreme type of female genital mutilation, involving excision of part or all of the external genitalia and stitching or narrowing of the vaginal opening
micronutrients	nutrients needed in very small amounts for normal growth and development, e.g., a vitamin or mineral
obstructed labour	labour in which despite strong contractions of the uterus, the fetus cannot descend through the pelvis because a barrier prevents its descent
opportunistic infections	infections that take advantage of weakness in the immune system such as caused by HIV
ORS	oral rehydration salts
PCP pneumonia	pneumocystis pneumonia – a common 'opportunistic' infection in children and people living (infected) with HIV
pentavalent vaccine	a five-in-one vaccine that combines the DTP (also referred to as DPT), HepB and Hib vaccines
***Plasmodium falciparum* malaria**	the most serious type of malaria, which causes nearly all malaria deaths
PMTCT	prevention of mother-to-child transmission of HIV
prolonged labour	labour with a duration of more than 24 hours
respiratory tract	the system in the body that takes in and distributes oxygen
STI	sexually transmitted infection
stillbirth	the birth of a fetus that has died in the womb